Cultivating a Compassionate Heart:
The Yoga Method of Chenrezig

Cultivating a Compassionate Heart:

THE YOGA METHOD OF CHENREZIG

Bhikshuni Thubten Chodron

SNOW LION PUBLICATIONS

ITHACA, NEW YORK • BOULDER, COLORADO

Snow Lion Publications
P. O. Box 6483
Ithaca, NY 14851 USA
(607) 273-8519
www.snowlionpub.com

Designed and Typeset by Gopa & Ted2, Inc.
Illustrations by Peter Green

Printed in USA on acid-free recycled paper.

ISBN-10 1-55939-242-8
ISBN-13 978-1-55939-242-6

Library of Congress Cataloging-in-Publication Data
Thubten Chodron, 1950-
    Cultivating a compassionate heart : the yoga method of Chenrezig /
Thubten Chodron.
        p. cm.
    Includes bibliographical references.
        ISBN-13: 978-1-55939-242-6 (alk. paper)
        ISBN-10: 1-55939-242-8 (alk. paper)
        1. Avalokiteśvara (Buddhist deity) 2. Spiritual life—Buddhism.
    I. Title.
        BQ4710.A8T49 2006
        294.3'4211—dc22
                                                                2005035573

Also by Thubten Chodron

Buddhism for Beginners (Snow Lion Publications)

Glimpse of Reality (with Dr. Alexander Berzin)

Guided Meditations on the Lamrim, the Gradual Path to Enlightenment (set of 14 CDs) (Dharma Friendship Foundation)

How to Free Your Mind: Tara the Liberator (Snow Lion Publications)

Open Heart, Clear Mind (Snow Lion Publications)

The Path to Happiness (Texas Buddhist Association)

Taming the Mind (Snow Lion Publications)

Working with Anger (Snow Lion Publications)

Books edited by Thubten Chodron

Blossoms of the Dharma: Living as a Buddhist Nun (North Atlantic Books, Berkeley, CA)

A Chat about Heruka, by Lama Zopa Rinpoche (Lama Yeshe Wisdom Archives)

A Chat about Yamantaka, by Lama Zopa Rinpoche (Lama Yeshe Wisdom Archives)

Choosing Simplicity: A Commentary on the Bhikshuni Pratimoksha, by Ven. Bhikshuni Master Wu Yin (Snow Lion Publications)

Heruka Body Mandala: Sadhana and Commentary, by Ven. Lati Rinpoche

Interfaith Insights (Timeless Books, New Delhi)

Pearl of Wisdom, Books I and II: Buddhist Prayers and Practices (Sravasti Abbey)

Transforming Adversity into Joy and Courage: An Explanation of the Thirty-seven Practices of Bodhisattvas, by Geshe Jampa Tegchok (Snow Lion Publications)

Contents

THE DALAI LAMA

Foreword

THE PROBLEMS THAT WE FACE as human beings today demand a positive mental attitude and a sense of compassion for others. I firmly believe we can solve the majority of our problems by developing a sense of universal responsibility, which is to want to do something for others without a selfish motive, out of a feeling of compassion. Moreover, the Tibetan word for this has the connotation of being courageously determined — not only thinking about others and wanting to do something for them, but actually putting these good wishes into effect.

All different religions have a special role to play in the awakening of compassion. They all realise the importance of compassion and have the potential to increase and enhance compassion and harmony. It is on the basis of this common potential that they can all understand each other and work together. On the other hand, I believe that qualities such as compassion and forgiveness are fundamental human qualities. They do not belong exclusively to religion. As a Buddhist, I believe religion evolves on the basis of our actual human nature. Religion strengthens and increases our natural positive qualities. Therefore, it is compassion rather than religion that is actually important to us. As sentient beings we are all dependent on one another, we do not exist in isolation. Therefore, as the great Indian sage Shantideva encouraged, we should help each other with the same eagerness as our hand pulls a thorn out of our foot.

The compassion of all the Buddhas appears in the form of Chenrezig, also known as Kuan Yin, Kannon, and Avalokiteshvara. I do the meditation practice of Chenrezig on a daily basis so that compassion may guide my life. However, simply praying to Chenrezig to make our hearts compassionate is not sufficient. We must practise the analytical or reflective meditations found in such valuable books as the *Stages of the Path to Enlightenment* (Lam-rim), the texts on Thought Transformation, or Mind Training, (Lo-jong), and Shantideva's *Guide to the Bodhisattva's Way of Life* (Bodhicharyavatara) that have been particularly effective in helping me develop whatever sense of compassion I may have.

I have no doubt that if we cultivate these analytical meditations and focus on developing *bodhichitta* — the aspiration to attain enlightenment for the benefit of all beings—in conjunction with the yoga method of Chenrezig, it will serve as an effective way to diminish our self-centeredness and open our hearts to others, as we generate compassion for them and for ourselves. I am confident that the twofold approach presented in this meditation manual of actively transforming the mind into compassion by means of reflective meditation, as well as by the visualization of Chenrezig and recitation of his mantra, has the potential to be particularly effective.

Over the many years that I have known her, Bhikshuni Thubten Chodron has often impressed me with her practical, clear-sighted, down to earth approach to spiritual practice. Just as carpenters or masons first prepare their tools and gather the necessary materials together before beginning whatever they are going to construct, so in this book she has assembled the instructions, inspiration, and advice from her own experience for cultivating a compassionate heart; what remains is for readers who are interested to put them into effect. I offer my prayers that all those who seek to apply them sincerely will be blessed with success, for the benefit of others and themselves.

October 26, 2005

Preface

My dear readers of this Chenrezig meditation
who are my brothers and sisters,

Chenrezig is the embodiment of all of the Buddhas' compassion. The
main function of this deity called Chenrezig is to develop compassion
in the hearts of oneself and all sentient beings. Compassion is the mind
that cares for others, whether they help you, harm you, or are indifferent. Why is it so important for us sentient beings to generate compassion in our hearts? Without compassion, this world would be a billion
times worse than it is now. With compassion, there will be less war,
famine, disease, torture, and natural disasters, all of which come from
karma.

Your mind creates karma. It all depends on you and how you think.
The correct way of thinking transforms activities into virtue, and the
result of these activities is only happiness. Thinking in a mistaken way
leads to engaging in nonvirtuous actions, which result only in suffering.
Living daily life with compassion for others is the purest attitude, and
thus your actions become the best virtue. These actions result in happiness and success now and in future lives, as well as freedom from the

oceans of samsaric suffering. These results include all that one wishes for: a good rebirth and the peerless happiness of enlightenment. If you live with an open heart, not closed tight with self-cherishing, your life is filled with positive things and joy. You do not have much regret now and even less at the time of death. You rejoice at goodness, and you will benefit others in this world, including animals. There are no barriers between you and others, and you feel everyone is connected and kind to you—others become precious to you, like family. When you feel and act like that, others will feel the same way about you—you will be dear to them, like family. They will care for you, love, support, and share with you, and your heart and life will be filled with light. By living with a good heart each day, you can say goodbye to depression as well as to the selfish mind from which depression comes.

Compassion brings peace in the world, in your country, and in your family. It brings harmony and peace between children and parents and couples. With compassion, all of your wishes for happiness will be fulfilled. Why? Because with compassion you help others be free from difficulties. As a result of the benefit you bring to others—freeing them from problems, others will help you fulfill your wishes. You will receive support from others dependent on your helping them; scientifically this is the nature of cause and effect. All this depends on us, no matter whether we are a Buddhist or a nonbeliever.

The opposite of compassion—the self-cherishing thought that renounces others' welfare and doesn't care about them—harms others. It leads you to harm so many sentient beings with your body, speech, and mind. From these actions (causes), you receive the effect—others harm you. Instead of happiness you continuously experience misery and problems. If we look at our lives and examine our experiences, we can see this very clearly. We can understand how a happy life and a suffering life are dependent on causes and conditions created by that individual. Think about this even if you are a nonbeliever and do not want to follow any religion. If you want happiness, practicing the good heart is essential.

Thus compassion is the root of all of happiness—the peerless happiness of enlightenment, the peace of being free from samsara, and the happiness of this life that we experience moment to moment. Without compassion, your life is filled with unending problems. Therefore compassion is the root of your own and all other living beings' happiness. So many sentient beings will be happy in this life by your being compassionate; your compassion also enables numberless other sentient beings to be happy in future lives, to attain freedom from samsara, and to become fully enlightened Buddhas.

Whether others practice compassion towards you or not, if you don't practice the good heart, you may harm other sentient beings throughout your life. One individual without compassion can make many millions of people suffer. That person can destroy the world, if not in this life, maybe in another life. Therefore practicing compassion is the most important meditation, the most important practice, and the best way to lead your life. For everyone—a leader of a country, a business person, a farmer, an actor, an enlisted man or woman, a worker, a married person, an ordained person, a doctor, a nurse, or a prostitute—compassion is the best way to live the life.

To develop compassion, prayers are not sufficient. Extensive intellectual understanding of philosophy is not enough. One needs to meditate. Yet even that is not enough. One needs to receive the special blessing of the Deity of Compassion, Chenrezig. Thus one needs to meditate on Chenrezig and recite the mantra of the Deity of Compassion, om mani padme hum. Om mani padme hum is the mantra cherished by all the Buddhas. By reciting this mantra you will be able to fulfill the wishes of all sentient beings. This mantra may be recited by anyone wishing for happiness, even the animals, mosquitoes, spiders, lobsters, and ants need to recite it, if they could!

The author of this meditation book, Ven. Thubten Chodron, has been a Dharma student since 1975. She was ordained as a sramanerika (getsulma) in 1977 and as a bhikshuni (gelongma) in 1986, and she has been teaching in different parts of the world for many years, awakening many sentient beings, giving light in their lives, saving them from the causes of suffering, and causing them to attain not only temporal but ultimate happiness. Her attitude and activities fit well with the Compassionate-Eyed Buddha, as well as the meaning of the mantra *om mani padme hum*—sincerely wishing, without conditions, to abandon the causes of suffering and practice virtue, which is the cause of all happiness up to enlightenment; benefiting others in many different ways: liberating prisoners from the real prison of samsara, the continuation of which has no beginning; effortlessly leading retreats for other people; tirelessly giving inspiring Dharma talks; leading courses in many different countries; creating a place for practice; being a good example— an inspiration for women in the world, by giving herself to others with full confidence.

Thank you very much to Chenrezig, to Ven. Chodron, and to people who read this text.

Sincerely,
Lama Zopa Rinpoche
30 July, 2005

Acknowledgments

CHENREZIG—Kuan Yin as s/he is known in China, Kannon in Japan, and Avalokiteshvara in the Sanskrit language—is the Buddha of Compassion, guiding us in the process of transforming our minds and hearts into those of a Buddha. From the depth of my heart, I pay homage to the Compassionate-Eyed One. Simultaneously, I express my respect and gratitude to His Holiness the Dalai Lama, Tsenzhap Serkong Rinpoche, Lama Thubten Yeshe, and Lama Zopa Rinpoche who taught me the invaluable practice of the Great Compassionate One. Without their teachings and guidance, the thought to do this book would never have arisen.

Lama Zopa Rinpoche wrote the general meditation on Thousand-Arm Chenrezig. The section "Those who have received the great empowerment into the Chenrezig mandala" was extracted from the Nyung Nä sadhana, written by the Seventh Dalai Lama. Master Chandrakirti wrote "A Lamentation Requesting Blessings from the Great Compassionate One," and Yangsi Rinpoche translated it from Tibetan into English with the help of Ven. Lhundrup Namdrol. The commentary is a compilation of talks I gave on the Chenrezig practice at Dharma Friendship Foundation in Seattle and at Cloud Mountain Retreat Center, as well as Q & A sessions during a one-month group retreat with Casa Tibet Mexico. I would like to thank Ven. Tenzin Tsepal for transcribing and lightly editing the talks and Peter Green for his inspiring drawings of Chenrezig. All mistakes are my own.

The Chenrezig practice is very rich. As I was preparing this book, so many more points about sutra and tantra came to mind to explain than could be included here. I encourage Buddhist practitioners to request qualified tantric masters to grant them the Chenrezig empowerment and give them extensive teachings on this practice, including teachings on the bodhisattva vows and the Action Tantra pledges. This commentary will get you going in practice, but it in no way compares to the commentaries of the great masters.

To do this practice in full—that is, meditating on the section entitled "Those who have received the great empowerment into the Chenrezig mandala"—one must have received the great empowerment (Tib: *wong*) of Thousand-Arm Chenrezig. Those who have not yet received this can do the practice by meditating on the section entitled "Those who have not received the great empowerment into the Chenrezig mandala" without self-generating as the deity. In whichever way we do this practice, making our minds closer to Chenrezig's mind by cultivating the same spiritual qualities and realizations as Chenrezig is a valuable and meaningful practice.

Bhikshuni Thubten Chodron
Sravasti Abbey
May 23, 2005

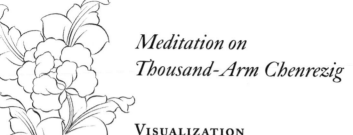

Meditation on Thousand-Arm Chenrezig

VISUALIZATION

IN THE SPACE in front of me is the divine form of Thousand-Arm Chenrezig, who is the embodiment of all the infinite Buddhas' compassionate wisdom. He stands on a lotus and moon seat. His body is in the nature of white light, youthful, and decorated with magnificent jewel ornaments.

He has eleven faces. Of the three on his shoulders, his center face is white, the right green, and the left red. Above those, his center face is green, the right red, and the left white. Above those, his center face is red, the right white, and the left green. Above those is a wrathful dark blue face with yellow hair standing erect. On the top of that is the red head of Amitabha Buddha, peaceful and smiling.

Chenrezig's first two hands are at his heart, palms together, holding a wish-fulfilling gem. On his right, the second hand holds a crystal rosary, reminding me to recite the mantra. The third hand is in the gesture of giving realizations and from it a rain of nectar falls, curing the hunger and thirst of the hungry ghosts. The fourth hand holds a Dharma wheel.

On his left, the second hand holds a golden lotus, the purest of flowers although it is born from the mud. The third hand holds a vase containing the nectar of his compassionate wisdom. The fourth holds a bow and arrow, symbolizing defeat of the four negative forces. The other 992 hands are in the gesture of giving the highest realizations. An antelope skin is draped over his left shoulder, hatred is overcome completely by peaceful, compassionate wisdom.

TAKING REFUGE AND GENERATING THE ALTRUISTIC INTENTION (BODHICITTA)

I take refuge until I am enlightened in the Buddha, the Dharma, and the Sangha. By the positive potential I create by practicing generosity and the other far-reaching attitudes (*paramitas*), may I attain Buddhahood in order to benefit all sentient beings. (Recite 3 times from the depth of your heart.)

THE FOUR IMMEASURABLES

How wonderful it would be if all sentient beings were to abide in equanimity, free of bias, attachment, and anger. May they abide in this way. I shall cause them to abide in this way. Guru Chenrezig, please inspire me to be able to do so.

How wonderful it would be if all sentient beings had happiness and its causes. May they have these. I shall cause them to have these. Guru Chenrezig, please inspire me to be able to do so.

How wonderful it would be if all sentient beings were free from suffering and its causes. May they be free. I shall cause them to be free. Guru Chenrezig, please inspire me to be able to do so.

How wonderful it would be if all sentient beings were never parted from upper rebirth and liberation's excellent bliss. May they never be parted. I shall cause them never to be parted. Guru Chenrezig, please inspire me to be able to do so.

THE SPECIAL ALTRUISTIC INTENTION

Especially for the sake of all mother sentient beings, I must quickly and more quickly, in this very life, attain the precious state of complete and perfect enlightenment. Therefore I shall practice the Guru Chenrezig Yoga Method.

Seven-Limb Prayer

Reverently I prostrate with my body, speech, and mind,
And present clouds of every type of offering, actual and mentally
  transformed.
I confess all my negative actions accumulated since beginningless
  time
And rejoice in the virtues of all holy and ordinary beings.
Please remain until cyclic existence ends
And turn the wheel of Dharma for sentient beings.
I dedicate all the virtues of myself and others to the great
  enlightenment.

Mandala Offering

This ground, anointed with perfume, flowers strewn,
Mount Meru, four lands, sun and moon,
Imagined as a Buddha-land and offered to you:
May all beings enjoy this pure land.

The objects of attachment, aversion, and ignorance—friends, enemies,
and strangers, my body, wealth, and enjoyments—I offer these without
any sense of loss. Please accept them with pleasure and inspire me and
others to be free from the three poisonous attitudes.

IDAM GURU RATNA MANDALAKAM NIRYATAYAMI

Request Prayer

O Arya Compassionate-Eyed One
Who is the treasure of compassion,
I request you, please listen to me,
Please guide myself, mothers, and fathers
In all six realms to be freed quickly

From the great ocean of samsara.
I request that the vast and profound
Peerless awakening mind may grow.
With the tear of your great compassion,
Please cleanse all karmas and delusions.
Please lead with your hand of compassion
Me and migrators to fields of bliss.
Please, Amitabha and Chenrezig,
In all my lives be virtuous friends.
Show well the undeceptive pure path
And quickly place us in Buddha's state.

MEDITATION ON
The Eight Verses of Thought Transformation

(After each verse, visualize much light coming from Chenrezig, flowing into you and completely filling your whole body. It purifies the selfishness and ignorance that prevent you from understanding the meaning of that verse and gives you the ability to understand and integrate each verse into your life. If you like, say the six-syllable mantra a few times while visualizing in this way.)

1.   With the thought of attaining enlightenment
     For the welfare of all beings,
     Who are more precious than a wish-fulfilling jewel,
     I will constantly practice holding them dear.

2.   Whenever I am with others
     I will practice seeing myself as the lowest of all,
     And from the very depth of my heart
     I will respectfully hold others as supreme.

3.   In all actions I will examine my mind,
     And the moment a disturbing attitude arises,

Endangering myself and others,
I will firmly confront and avert it.

4. Whenever I meet a person of bad nature
    Who is overwhelmed by negative energy and intense suffering,
    I will hold such a rare one dear,
    As if I had found a precious treasure.

5. When others, out of jealousy,
    Mistreat me with abuse, slander, and so on,
    I will practice accepting defeat
    And offering the victory to them.

6. When someone I have benefited
    And in whom I have placed great trust
    Hurts me very badly,
    I will practice seeing that person as my supreme teacher.

7. In short, I will offer directly and indirectly
    Every benefit and happiness to all beings, my mothers.
    I will practice in secret taking upon myself
    All their harmful actions and sufferings.

8. Without these practices being defiled by the stains of the
        eight worldly concerns,
    By perceiving all phenomena as illusory,
    I will practice without grasping to release all beings
    From the bondage of the disturbing unsubdued mind and karma.

*Those who have not received the great empowerment
into the Chenrezig mandala*
*(If you have not received the great empowerment into the Chenrezig mandala,
continue with the front generation, doing the purification and absorption
below. Then go to the dedication verses at the end of the sadhana. Those doing*

the self-generation may skip the purification and absorption below and go to the section entitled "Those who have received the great empowerment into the Chenrezig mandala" and continue from there to the end of the sadhana.)

PURIFICATION AND RECEIVING INSPIRATION

Chenrezig now comes on top of my head, facing the same direction as I do. Chenrezig also appears on the heads of all sentient beings, who are seated around me. At the heart of each Chenrezig are a lotus and flat moon disk. Standing at the center of the moon is the seed syllable HRIH, the essence of Chenrezig's omniscient mind of wisdom and compassion. This is surrounded by the syllables of the long mantra, and inside this stand the syllables of the six-syllable mantra. All is made of radiant light.

From the mantra syllables and HRIH much white light and nectar, representing the nature of Chenrezig's blissful omniscient mind, flow into me, permeating my entire nervous system. They totally purify all disturbing attitudes, negative karmic imprints, diseases, and obscurations. I feel completely pure and blissful. The light and nectar also fill me with all the realizations of the gradual path to enlightenment, especially Chenrezig's love, compassion, and wisdom.

Similarly, light and nectar from the Chenrezigs on the crowns of all the sentient beings flow into them, purifying all negativities and obscurations and inspiring them with all the realizations of the path to enlightenment. *(Do this visualization while reciting the long mantra and then the six-syllable mantra.)*

Long mantra in Sanskrit:
NAMO RATNA TRAYAYA / NAMAH ARYA JÑANA SAGARA / VAIROCHANA VYUHA RAJAYA / TATHAGATAYA / ARHATE / SAMYAK SAMBUDDHAYA / NAMAH SARVA TATHAGATEBHYAH/ ARHATE-BHYAH / SAMYAK SAMBUDDHEBHYAH / NAMAH ARYA AVALOKI-TESHVARAYA / BODHISATTVAYA / MAHASATTVAYA / MAHA KARUNIKAYA / TADYATHA / OM DHARA DHARA / DHIRI DHIRI /

DHURU DHURU / ITTE VATTE / CHALE CHALE / PRACHALE
PRACHALE / KUSUME KUSUME VARE / ILI MILI / CHITI JVALAM /
APANAYE SVAHA

Long mantra as pronounced by Tibetans:
*namo ratna trayaya/ nama arya gyana sagara/ berotsana buha radzaya/
tatagataya/ arhate/ samyaksam buddhaya/ namo sarwa tatagatebhye/
arhatebhye/ samyaksam buddhebhye/ namo arya awalokite/ shoraya/ bodhi
satoya/ maha satoya/ maha karunikaya/ tayata/ om/ dara dara/ diri diri/
duru duru/ itte wate/ tsale tsale/ partsale partsale/ kusume kusume ware/ ihli
mili/ tsiti dzola/ ahpanaye soha/*

Six-syllable mantra in Sanskrit:
OM MANI PADME HUM

Six-syllable mantra as pronounced by Tibetans:
Om mani pay may hung

ABSORPTION

I will live my life in a meaningful way, and do all actions with the moti-
vation to attain enlightenment for the benefit of all sentient beings.
Because I have such a noble intention, Chenrezig is extremely pleased.
He melts into white light and absorbs into my heart.

By Chenrezig absorbing into me, my mind becomes the nature of
great compassion, loving-kindness, and bodhicitta. My body is filled
with light and becomes very pure and clear, like crystal. *(Concentrate on
this for a while.)*

The Chenrezigs on the heads of all the sentient beings melt into
light, absorb into them, and bless them so that they may progress along
the gradual path to enlightenment.

*(Now dedicate the positive potential from doing the meditation by reciting
the dedication prayers at the end of the sadhana.)*

Those who have received the great empowerment into the Chenrezig mandala
(Do the self-generation practice of the six deities as follows.)

1. Ultimate Nature of the Deity (meditation on emptiness)

OM SVABHAVA SHUDDHA SARVA DHARMA SVABHAVA SHUDDHO HAM
(OM by essential nature all phenomena are pure; by essential nature I am pure.)

The nature of myself, of the meditational deity, and of all phenomena is pure in the one taste of emptiness.

2. Deity of Sound

Within the sphere of emptiness, the aspect of the tone of the mantra OM MANI PADME HUM resonates, pervading the realm of space.

3. Deity of Letter

The ultimate nature of the deity is inseparable from the transcendental aspect of my own mind. This manifests as a moon mandala. Above that, the sound of the mantra resonating in space manifests around the moon in the aspect of written letters, which are like very pure and bright mercury mixing completely with grains of gold.

4. Deity of Form

That transforms into a thousand-petal lotus, glittering with brilliant light. Its center is decorated with OM MANI PADME HUM. Infinite light radiates from the lotus, moon, and mantra letters, presenting clouds of offerings to all the Buddhas and bodhisattvas. They bestow blessings and inspiration of their body, speech, and mind, and the light reabsorbs.

Again light radiates. On the tip of each ray is the Superior, the Great Compassionate One, going out to purify and empower the sentient beings. A great cloud is emanated and from it a rain of nectar falls, pacifying the sufferings of sentient beings. All sentient beings are satisfied with bliss and become Chenrezig. All of these Chenrezigs absorb back into my mind, which is in the form of the lotus, moon, and mantra garland.

These transform into a variegated lotus and moon seat. Above that I arise as Chenrezig, white, youthful, radiating, and beautiful. I have eleven faces. Of the three on my shoulders, the center face is white, the right green, and the left red. Above those, my center face is green, the right red, and the left white. Above those, my center face is red, the right white, and the left green. All of the faces have fine, narrow eyes and are smiling. Above those is a snarling, wrathful dark blue face with three eyes and yellow hair standing erect. On top of that is the red head of Amitabha Buddha, in the form of a monk, peaceful and smiling.

My first two hands are at my heart, palms together, holding a wish-fulfilling gem. On my right, the second hand holds a crystal rosary. The third hand is in the gesture of giving realizations and from it a rain of nectar falls, curing the hunger and thirst of the hungry ghosts. The fourth hand holds a Dharma wheel.

On my left, the second hand holds a golden lotus. The third hand holds a vase with nectar. The fourth holds a bow and arrow. The other 992 hands, soft like lotus petals, are in the gesture of giving the highest realizations. In the palm of each hand is an eye. The hands do not extend beyond the crown pinnacle or below the knees. An antelope skin is draped over my left shoulder. I am adorned with a skirt made of the finest cloth, a golden belt decorated with jewels, a jeweled crown, earrings, necklace, armlets, anklets, and scarves of different colors. My red-yellow hair is arranged in garlands.

At my crown is a white OM, at my throat, a red AH, at my heart, a blue HUM. At my heart is a moon disk with the white syllable HRIH.

5. Deity of Mudra

OM PADMA UDBHAVAYE SVAHA

(With the mudra of the lotus essence, touch your hands to your heart, brow, neck, and right and left shoulders. Say this mantra while touching each point.)

6. Deity of Sign

At my heart is a moon disk. Seated on that is the transcendental wisdom being, white Chenrezig, with one face and two arms. His right hand is in the mudra of giving sublime realizations and the left is holding a lotus at the heart. At his heart is a moon disk. On that is the concentration being, the white syllable HRIH. The HRIH is surrounded by the letters of the long mantra, and inside this stand the letters of the six-syllable mantra.

(Meditate to develop clear appearance of yourself as Chenrezig and divine identity of being Chenrezig:

Clear appearance of yourself as the deity. *Go over the details of your Chenrezig body and then concentrate single-pointedly on this image of yourself as Chenrezig. Doing this overcomes the ordinary appearance of yourself as an ordinary being trapped in cyclic existence. Don't think that your ordinary body has become Chenrezig, because your ordinary body of flesh and bones vanished when you meditated on emptiness; your wisdom realizing emptiness now appears in the form of Chenrezig.*

Divine identity (divine dignity or divine pride). *By concentrating on the feeling "I am the Buddha Chenrezig," you will overcome ordinary grasping that holds onto a poor-quality image of yourself and grasping at yourself as inherently existent. An inherently existent "I" doesn't become Chenrezig—it can't because such an "I" doesn't exist at all. Rather, your conventional "I" becomes Chenrezig.*

Then, aware that the two—appearance and emptiness—arise together, meditate on the yoga of nondual profundity and clarity. Clarity is concentrating on having the body of the deity; profundity is the wisdom knowing this body and self are empty of inherent existence. Try to unify method and wisdom in one consciousness; that is, meditate that your wisdom realizing emptiness (wisdom) assumes the appearance of the deity (method). Thus, while you appear as Chenrezig, ascertain that you are empty of inherent existence.

While you are empty, you appear as Chenrezig. Chenrezig is like a reflection or an illusion, appearing in one way but existing in another. Chenrezig is a dependent arising, dependent on the basis of designation, name, and concept.)

Mantra Recitation

At my heart is a white moon and the concentration being HRIH. Surrounding this, standing clockwise on the moon, are the syllables of the long mantra, white in color. Inside this stand the syllables of the six-syllable mantra. Light radiates from these and completely fills my body. All obscurations, diseases, and hindrances are purified. The light radiates outside, carrying a countless number of Great Compassionate Ones. They purify all sentient beings' negative karma, disturbing attitudes, negative emotions, and obscurations.

The light gives sentient beings all the temporal happiness they want. It also ripens their minds so that they receive the realizations of the gradual path to enlightenment and attain the ultimate happiness of Buddhahood. All sentient beings become Chenrezig.

Again, light rays radiate from my heart. They carry offerings to all the Buddhas and to all the sentient beings who have become Chenrezig. All these Chenrezigs are extremely pleased and experience bliss. Then all the qualities of Chenrezig's holy body, speech, and mind in the form of white light come from all the Chenrezigs and absorb into my heart, blessing my mind. All the Buddhas and all the sentient beings who have become Chenrezigs fall like snowflakes into me. I feel very blissful and my body, speech, and mind become inseparable from Guru Chenrezig's holy body, speech, and mind.

(While doing the above visualizations, recite the long mantra and the six-syllable mantra.)

Long mantra in Sanskrit:

NAMO RATNA TRAYAYA / NAMAH ARYA JÑANA SAGARA /
VAIROCHANA VYUHA RAJAYA / TATHAGATAYA / ARHATE / SAMYAK
SAMBUDDHAYA / NAMAH SARVA TATHAGATEBHYAH/ ARHATE-
BHYAH / SAMYAK SAMBUDDHEBHYAH / NAMAH ARYA AVALOKITESH-
VARAYA / BODHISATTVAYA / MAHASATTVAYA / MAHA KARUNIKAYA
/ TADYATHA / OM DHARA DHARA / DHIRI DHIRI / DHURU DHURU /
ITTE VATTE / CHALE CHALE / PRACHALE PRACHALE / KUSUME
KUSUME VARE / ILI MILI / CHITI JVALAM / APANAYE SVAHA

Long mantra as pronounced by Tibetans:

*namo ratna trayaya/ nama arya gyana sagara/ berotsana buha radzaya/
tatagataya/ arhate/ samyaksam buddhaya/ namo sarwa tatagatebhye/
arhatebhye/ samyaksam buddhebhye/ namo arya awalokite/ shoraya/ bodhi
satoya/ maha satoya/ maha karunikaya/ tayata/ om/ dara dara/ diri diri/
duru duru/ itte wate/ tsale tsale/ partsale partsale/ kusume kusume ware/ ihli
mili/ tsiti dzola/ ahpanaye soha/*

Six-syllable mantra in Sanskrit:

OM MANI PADME HUM

Six-syllable mantra as pronounced by Tibetans:

Om mani pay may hung

*(Visualize Vajrasattva on your crown. Nectar flows from his heart into you,
purifying any incorrect mantra recitations. Recite the following one-hun-
dred-syllable Vajrasattva mantra 3x.)*

OM PADMASATTVA SAMAYA MANUPALAYA / PADMASATTVA
TVENOPATHISHTHA / DRIDHO ME BHAVA / SUTOSHYO MAY
BHAVA / SUPOSHYO ME BHAVA / ANURAKTO ME BHAVA / SARVA
SIDDHIM ME PRAYACCHA / SARVA KARMA SUCHAME / CHITTAM
SHRIYAM KURU HUM / HA HA HA HA HOH / BHAGAVAN / SARVA
TATHAGATA / PADMA MAME MUNCHA / PADMA BHAVA MAHA
SAMAYA SATTVA AH HUM PHAT

Becoming the Simple Form of Chenrezig

All my faces absorb into the root face, all the arms into the root arms. I maintain the divine dignity of myself as the Great Compassionate One, with one face and two arms, with an OM at my crown, AH at my throat, and HUM at my heart.

Dedication

Due to this merit may we soon
Attain the enlightened state of Chenrezig
That we may be able to liberate
All sentient beings from their sufferings.

May the precious bodhi mind
Not yet born arise and grow.
May that born have no decline
But increase forever more.

Due to the positive potentials accumulated by myself and others in the past, present, and future, may anyone who merely sees, hears, remembers, touches, or talks to me be freed in that very instant from all sufferings and abide in happiness forever.

In all rebirths, may I and all sentient beings be born in a good family, have clear wisdom and great compassion, be free of pride and be devoted to our spiritual masters, and abide within the vows and commitments to our spiritual masters.

In whatever guise you appear, O Chenrezig, whatever your retinue, life span, and pure land, whatever your name most noble and holy, may I and all others attain only these.

By the force of these praises and requests made to you, may all disease, poverty, fighting, and quarrels be calmed. May the Dharma and all auspiciousness increase throughout the worlds and directions where I and all others dwell.

In the snowy mountain paradise
You're the source of good and happiness.
Powerful Tenzin Gyatso, Chenrezig,
May you stay until samsara ends.

DAILY ACTIVITIES

When you are doing your daily activities, visualize yourself as Chenrezig and the environment and beings around you as Chenrezig's pure land inhabited by many Chenrezigs. When you eat or enjoy other sense pleasures, offer them to Chenrezig. Whenever you are praised, think the praise is directed to Chenrezig.

A Lamentation Requesting Blessings from the Great Compassionate One

By Master Chandrakirti

I prostrate to the all-mighty bodhisattva Chenrezig

Arya Chenrezig, great compassionate one,
Your perfect body the color of a stainless conch,
Beautified by a pure, luminous moon disk
Like a thousand rays of sun shining in the sky,
Overshadowing the brilliant light of the dakas;
Renowned as the teacher and guide of the beings of the three realms
    of existence,
You are the single friend of all migratory beings;
Loving compassionate protector deity, please consider me.

From beginningless time, I have wandered
In cyclic existence, on mistaken and abandoned paths,
Erring due to mistakes and nonvirtues of the past;
I deeply regret and feel sorrow for all of my misdeeds.

By the force of my egotistical actions
I am sinking in the ocean of cyclic suffering,
The blazing fire of anger burning my mind,
The accumulated darkness of ignorance obscuring my wisdom.

My consciousness is submerged in the ocean of attachment;
The mountain of great pride forces me down to the lower realms;
The swirling winds of jealousy distract me in samsara;
I am bound by the tight knots of egotistical view.

Fallen into this pit of desire, like a well of burning coals,
The mire of violent suffering falls like rain;
The fire element, the scorching sun, burns from above;
The water element, the moisture of the earth, brings cold from
    below.
Outside the bitter cold burns;
Raging winds terrorize me to the depths of my heart.

This suffering is intensely difficult to bear—
How can you restrain yourself?
All of this suffering I have confronted,
Never abandoning aspiring faith for you.
Supreme arya, noble protector, how could you think not to
    benefit beings?

Loving protector, why won't you show me compassion?
Miserable by reason of birth, I am weary of karma.
Though despondent from fatigue, the force of karma cannot be
    changed.
Its impetus is like a stream of water
And, like a hurricane, the power of karma is extremely difficult to
    reverse.
These hardships are difficult to express

My body, speech, and mind come under the command of nonvirtue.
By the force of the fierce burning fire of negative karma
The miserable result of consciousness arises.
If the aggregates, this body of illusion, cannot bear this,
Loving protector Chenrezig, can you bear it?

When I seek to see the Compassionate One's face,
Luminous like the sun, lustrous like the moon,
I cannot see with eyes afflicted
By the eye disease of beginningless ignorance.
Protector of the world, where are you now?
Unable to tolerate this terrible suffering,
Reeling from the panic of extreme terror and fear,
I utter this longing lamentation,
A miserable, desperate plea for help.
Loving protector Chenrezig, how can you bear it?

When, at the time of death, I change my body,
I will be separated from friends and relatives, taken by the Lord
    of Death.
My worldly relatives will not want to let me go,
But due to the power of karma, I will be taken alone.
If, at that time, no refuge exists for me,
Will you, loving protector, dismiss me into samsara?

A being like me, oppressed by karma,
Due to wrong prayers from beginningless time,
Has not yet been released from the three realms, the place
    of samsara.
As many times as I have taken rebirth over countless eons,
Taking countless bodies that fell apart,
If I collected the flesh and bones, they would fill the world;
If I collected the pus and blood, it would equal the great ocean.
But if I consider what remains of my karma, it is beyond thought,
    inexpressible.

Although I have passed through the three realms countless times,
All of my actions have been a meaningless waste.
Among all of my possibly existent countless rebirths,
If there was even one in which

I completed a single action towards the unsurpassable purpose of
   enlightenment,
From doing only that there would have been some meaning.

Karma is powerful. Due to the great force of the afflictions,
Beings take bodies of flesh and blood and wander in samsara,
Caught in the wretched misery of the prison of existence.
Due to my wrongdoings all of this fierce, inexhaustible suffering
Arises from my own actions.
I request you, with your great compassion, to cut this continuum
And destroy the winds of afflictions and karma.

As I wander perpetually in the darkness of ignorance
By the power of the winds of afflictions and karma,
Can't you see with the rays of your lamp of wisdom?
Since I cannot endure the results of my wrong actions,
Won't you carry out your compassionate enlightened activity?
Since I suffer the sickness of the three poisons, so difficult to bear,
Won't you heal me with the skillful medicine of compassion?
Since I plummet from the cliff of wrong views,
Won't you catch me with your compassionate hand?
Since I burn in the great suffering fire of karma,
Won't you allow the cooling continuum of the water of your
   compassion to fall upon me?

Once I have purified my karma in the three realms of cyclic existence
   and obtained my goal,
At that time your great compassion will be of no benefit to me.
If you disregard the karmic propensities of sentient beings,
For whom will your great compassion act?
You, supreme tamer of beings, endowed with the power of
   compassion,
Please don't be careless, indifferent, or lazy.
Compassionate victor, from your heart, look upon me!

Colophon:

Translated by Yangsi Rinpoche with Ven. Tenzin Namdrol at Deer Park Buddhist Center, Madison, Wisconsin, August 2001.

Commentary on the
Yoga Method of Chenrezig

I *Getting Started*

CHENREZIG is our best friend. Think about it: Could we have a better friend than the Great Compassionate One? Is there anyone who could care about us more or help us more? But as with all friendships, we have to cultivate the relationship. We can't just take it for granted. So our daily meditation on Chenrezig is like touching base with our best friend every day, and doing Chenrezig retreat is like going on vacation with the one we love the most. It's something we take delight in and appreciate.

This sadhana is based on one compiled by Lama Zopa Rinpoche. In it is inserted the self-generation practice from the Nyung Nä sadhana, the text used during the two-day fasting retreat of Thousand-Arm Chenrezig. This way we can do a practice that has all the important elements of a front generation practice, in which we visualize the deity in front of us or above our heads, and the self-generation practice, in which we dissolve into emptiness and generate ourselves as the deity.

Before we go into the details of the practice, let's cultivate a good motivation for learning the Chenrezig practice—a motivation of love, compassion, and altruism for all sentient beings. Chenrezig's essence is compassion. We can't become close to Chenrezig or transform our mind into Chenrezig's if we are angry, jealous, competitive, or resentful of others. Thus, to make our mind into a good field in which the seeds of compassion can grow, the masters recommend that we follow four guidelines for practitioners of the Chenrezig Yoga Method.

Although these four sound simple, they are difficult and may even be considered "ascetic" practices.

1. Avoid insulting others when they insult us.
2. Avoid getting angry when others are angry at us.
3. Avoid beating others when they hit us.
4. Avoid observing others' faults when they observe ours.

For some people, these four practices are totally opposite to what they have been brought up to do. From the time they're little, they have been told that when another child hits them, they should strike them back in order to protect themselves and avoid more harm. Our national "security" is based on such a belief. In addition, when someone is angry at us, anger towards them seems to arise automatically in us, and when we're insulted or our faults are pointed out, we feel entitled to humiliate the other person by making them look bad in front of others.

Does this policy of retaliation bring us the peace we seek or does it escalate the conflict? Even if we trounce the other person and get even, do we feel good about ourselves, or is there a subtle—or not so subtle—feeling of guilt? Sure, we may sometimes feel proud and powerful when we get even, but how much of that feeling is due to an adrenaline rush and how much is due to genuine self-respect? In short, is revenge an effective strategy for solving difficulties among human beings on the personal, national, or international level? These are questions for you to contemplate. Please honestly examine your own life experience.

I work with prisoners, teaching them the Dharma and offering spiritual guidance. Many of them are incarcerated because of anger: they insulted, criticized, beat, and even killed others. I'd like to share with you a few stories that the inmates told me about working with anger and the instinct to retaliate.

Bo wrote:

I'm one of a few inmates allowed to take college courses. A few days ago, I was in my business management class, getting ready to take the final exam, when the woman next to me pointed to the person sitting in front of us, and said, "During the midterm a few weeks ago, I saw her cheating, using some notes she had. That makes me so mad! Does it make you as mad as it makes me?"

"That's on her," I replied. "If I let every person sitting in the classroom 'make me mad,' I wouldn't have any time to learn anything. She's just cheating herself anyway. After twelve years of being incarcerated, very little actually makes me really mad. I try not to give other people the power to make me mad. I'm the one who makes myself mad when I give someone else that power."

I've learned that anger is generated within. It's not the result of exterior phenomena; it is the result of our response to the things that run contrary to our likes and dislikes. Nothing that anyone can do to me can make me mad. I make myself crazy with anger. It originates inside me.

The world throws many things our way and how we respond to them is the issue. Can we bring the loving-kindness and the compassion that the Buddha taught is inside all of us to the forefront when it is most needed? This can be hard. My anger has suppressed much of my other feelings. It has commandeered my consciousness and has served to increase the pain and sufferings of this samsaric existence.

When we have the option of feeling compassion, love, and understanding, why do we abandon them to dwell in the pain and suffering of our anger? Why do we prefer that at times? It seems we find some kind of twisted sanctuary in our anger. Like a pig in mud, we wallow in it, and it clings to us, sometimes penetrating every pore of our consciousness. Why do we find this weird, dysfunctional comfort in anger? Do we need to be "right" all the time, so someone else must be wrong? Does our pride and arrogance of self have to be placated and coddled every minute?

I guess there is much about anger that I am only beginning to understand, but I've seen that anger is directly related to attachment. The more attached I am, the angrier I become when I can't get what I want. My anger is a result of having all those attachments.

Bryan told me:

I was thinking about how quickly we can become violent. A large percentage of the time it is over something trivial. We assume a posture that we believe we are supposed to maintain. If anyone exposes a chink in our armor or if we accidentally let our mask slip, we immediately become hostile and defensive. Two recent incidents made me examine how we view things.

One of them was the kidnapping and murder of the eleven-year-old girl in Florida. Almost everyone was saddened by the loss of such a young life. It was a shame that she (and her family) had so much taken from them. However, our sadness and compassion are displayed as outrage. Instead of saying prayers for the little girl and her family, we seek retribution and revenge from her murderer. We no longer focus on her innocence; we only see his guilt. No one around me has been talking about her or the feelings that this tragedy brought up in us. All we talk about is the anger and what we would like to do or see done to the man that stole her life. I wonder why is it so much easier for us to show our anger than it is to show our sympathy and love?

In the second incident, a little girl from the Dominican Republic was born with two heads. We all followed her surgery and were happy when it looked like she was going to recover. When she died, we were genuinely sad. There was no bad guy, no one for us to blame. We embraced our feelings because there was no one for us to point a finger at. There was no need for us to be hard or mean. In both of these cases, a child died, but in one, people let their anger overwhelm them and in the other they allowed their human empathy to come out. How strange we act!

To do these four practices of nonretaliation well, we must repeatedly do the meditations for generating bodhicitta. This may be done through following either the seven-point instruction of cause and effect or the system of equalizing and exchanging self and others. Both of these are thoroughly explained in Geshe Jampa Tegchok's book *Transforming Adversity into Joy and Courage*, which I recommend highly.

In addition, patience is a key practice. With it, we'll be able to subdue the anger that causes us to insult others, get angry at them, physically harm them, and observe their faults. *Working with Anger* and the sixth chapter of *A Guide to the Bodhisattva's Way of Life* by Shantideva spell out methods to subdue our anger in a healthy way.

GETTING READY

To prepare our mind before beginning the Chenrezig sadhana, clean the room, set up the altar, and make offerings. Then sit in a comfortable position. For this, the masters recommend the eight-point position of Vairochana:

1. The legs are crossed in the full vajra position, or half vajra. Since many people cannot sit in that position for a long time, sit on a cushion on the floor in a way that is comfortable for you. If you cannot do that, sit in a straight-backed chair with your feet flat on the floor.
2. The hands are in your lap, close to your body, with the right hand on top of the left, palms up and the thumbs touching to form a triangle.
3. The back is straight.
4. The mouth is closed with the tip of the tongue on the upper palate. Of course, if your nose is stuffed due to allergies or a cold, it's fine to open your mouth and breathe!
5. The head is upright or barely inclined.
6. The eyes are slightly open, allowing in some light although you are not looking at anything. This prevents distraction. Until you

memorize the sadhana, open your eyes to read it and then lower them again to contemplate the meaning.

7. The shoulders are level.

8. The mind is neutral, free from any strong emotions or preoccupying thoughts. When we sit down to meditate, sometimes our mind is dull because we've just woken up in the morning or it is stirred up due to being busy during the day. In the first case, doing some prostrations is helpful to energize the body and mind. In the second case, breathing meditation will clear away extraneous thoughts and enable the mind to settle down.

FRONT VISUALIZATION

To begin this practice, we visualize Chenrezig, take refuge, and cultivate a bodhicitta motivation. Like most sadhanas, this one begins with the description of the front generation so that the aspirations and positive thoughts we generate in subsequent verses are cultivated in the presence of an enlightened one. If we don't imagine Chenrezig, it could seem that we are taking refuge in empty space or in nothing in particular. However, by visualizing Chenrezig and thinking of him as the embodiment of the Three Jewels, we are clear about the direction we're taking in our spiritual practice and who we're entrusting to lead us there.

Then we cultivate bodhicitta and reinforce this by meditating on the four immeasurables. By doing this, we know why we are going in that direction. It will be hard to get anywhere in our spiritual practice if we don't know in what direction we're going and why we're going there. That's why we always begin with refuge and bodhicitta.

The sadhana opens with a description of Chenrezig so that we will know how to visualize him. Visualization doesn't mean seeing Chenrezig with our eyes. It means we have a mental image of him in our minds. For example, if someone says, "pizza," you have a clear image of a delicious pizza in your mind. When you think of a friend, a clear mental image of that person appears in your mind, even when your eyes are open. That's visualization. We may wonder why it's so easy for us to visualize pizza and so difficult to imagine Chenrezig. That's because we're more familiar with pizza and other objects of attachment, so they come to mind easily. We're comparatively unfamiliar with Chenrezig, so that visualization takes time to cultivate. However, as we make friends with Chenrezig and become familiar with him, the image of him will easily appear in our mind's eye.

One advantage of doing formal meditation sessions is that distracting external stimuli are restricted, enabling us to concentrate and visualize better. For this reason, we lower our eyes and sit in the meditation position in a quiet place. It's also beneficial to visualize Chenrezig when our eyes are open and we're doing things during the break time between meditation sessions.

Visualize Chenrezig about an arm's length or a body's length in front of you at eye level. The visualization is completely made of light, so don't think of an inanimate painting or a statue. Chenrezig is alive, vibrant, someone we can communicate with. He's not flat or static.

We can relate to Chenrezig in different ways. First, we can think of Chenrezig as an individual who did what we aspire to do—go from the ordinary state to the enlightened one. Second, we can see Chenrezig as a manifestation of all enlightened qualities. In this respect, it's very helpful to study the qualities of the Buddha as described in the refuge chapter of the Lamrim or in *The Ornament for Clear Realization*. The more familiar we are with a Buddha's qualities, the easier it will be to get a feeling for Chenrezig when we visualize him, because we imagine those qualities manifesting in the physical form of Chenrezig. Third, we can view Chenrezig as the manifestation of the enlightened being we will become. That is, Chenrezig is the Buddha that we will become in the future. He is our future Buddha appearing before us right now. Chenrezig is our Buddha-nature in its fully purified and evolved form. Depending upon what our practice needs at any particular moment, we can relate to Chenrezig in any of these ways.

Although we review the details of Chenrezig's appearance when we visualize him, the main point is to feel that we're in his presence—to experience being in the presence of incredible compassion, to feel that someone accepts us totally, without any judgment, and is committed to helping us become enlightened. One day, after I'd been doing this practice for many years, I realized that I had never imagined Chenrezig looking at me with complete compassion and acceptance because I couldn't imagine *anyone* looking at me that way. At that point, I saw how much I judged myself—and everyone else as well. After that, I started focusing in meditation on Chenrezig looking at me with compassion and acceptance. I tried to get used to the feeling of being looked at in that way. Over time this had a profound effect on me.

Sometimes we are so hard on ourselves that we can't imagine anyone else being any less critical of us than we are of ourselves. But Chenrezig doesn't look at us and think, "You think you're meditating? What a joke! You're distracted again, dreaming about pizza instead of thinking about me!" We don't need to think of ourselves in such a harsh light or assume that anyone else is thinking of us like that either.

Chenrezig is made of light and has one thousand arms. He is the embodiment of all the Buddhas, all the Dharma, all the Sangha. One way to think is that Chenrezig's body represents all the Sangha; his speech, all the Dharma; his mind, all the Buddhas. He's standing on top of a lotus and a flat moon seat—both of these are horizontal. The lotus represents renunciation—the determination to be free from samsara—and the moon seat symbolizes bodhicitta.

Chenrezig's body is made of white light; he is sixteen years old, very youthful. He's very beautiful, so your mind is naturally attracted to him. You could think about him forever, just like you think of your boyfriend or girlfriend without getting distracted! He's wearing jeweled ornaments, which symbolize the six far-reaching attitudes (Skt: *paramitas*). I've seen some teenagers on the Avenue wearing belts made of bullet casings. That shows their inner attitude; it conveys a message to everyone. Chenrezig wears jewels that convey another message: one of enlightenment.

He has eleven faces. There are three rows of three. On the first level, the center face is white; on his right (that means as you're looking at him, on your left) the face is green, and on the left (your right), red. Above those the center face is green, the one on his right is red, and the left one is white. Above those, his center face is red, the right white, and the left green. I've never heard an explanation of why his faces are these colors and why they are in this order. Above those is Vajrapani, a wrathful emanation of compassion, appearing as a dark blue, fierce face with yellow hair standing upward. Above that is the red head of Amitabha, peaceful and smiling. Here, Amitabha is in the form of a monk so he doesn't wear ornaments. Amitabha is the head of the Lotus Buddha-family, to which Chenrezig belongs. Chenrezig is one of the two main bodhisattvas in Sukhavati (Tib: *Dewa Chen*), Amitabha's pure land. These two bodhisattvas welcome those who are born there, but I don't think they stand at the gate saying, "Hi. Come on in. We've been waiting for you!" When people talk about seeing the Buddhas and going to the pure land, I'm not convinced that it's an external physical place that could be found on MapQuest. It seems to me that it's created by the mind. To be reborn there is dependent on our state of mind—our faith and confidence, bodhicitta, understanding of emptiness, concentration, and the purity of our vision.

Chenrezig's first two hands are at his heart, in the gesture we make when bowing—our palms together with the thumbs tucked in. The empty space around the thumbs represents the empty nature of the mind, the Buddha-nature. He's holding a wish-fulfilling gem, a jewel that grants all the wishes made by its owner. In this case, the wishes are for sentient beings to have happiness and its causes and to be free from all suffering and its causes. On his right, the second hand holds a rosary made of crystal. When doing Chenrezig retreat, it's good to use a crystal rosary or a bodhi seed rosary, if possible. By holding the rosary, he reminds us to recite the mantra. Also, thinking of a rosary can help us meditate on emptiness because it's clear that a rosary is composed of parts—beads and a string—and is merely labeled in dependence on those parts.

When the text speaks of "the third hand," it doesn't mean the next one down. Here the third hand is the lowest of the hands in that first row. That hand is in the gesture of giving realizations, so the palm is open outward and from it nectar rains down, eliminating the hunger and thirst of the hungry ghosts, those beings who suffer from painful dissatisfaction. We might think, "The hungry ghost realm is too strange. I don't know if I really believe in the existence of all these other realms." If we have trouble taking the existence of hungry ghosts seriously, we can remember that there are many people starving on this planet. Or, we can think of our own dissatisfied mind running here and there seeking pleasure. That's the mind of a hungry ghost, always dissatisfied, always grasping and craving, continually needy, and full of self-pity and frustration. The nectar flowing from Chenrezig's outstretched hand cures those ailments when they manifest physically or mentally. In the Chinese tradition, Chenrezig, or Kuan Yin, is usually female. Often she is depicted holding a vase filled with nectar that cures the suffering of sentient beings.

The fourth hand, which is the one in the middle, holds a Dharma wheel, symbolizing giving the teachings. Giving the Buddha's teachings is called "turning the Dharma wheel" because it sets the teachings in motion in our world and in sentient beings' minds.

On Chenrezig's left side, the second hand holds a golden lotus, which symbolizes bodhicitta. Just as a lotus is rooted in mud but remains unstained by it, so a bodhisattva resides in samsara but is not polluted by it. The third hand, which is the lowest one, holds a vase containing the nectar of his compassionate wisdom. The fourth holds a bow and arrow, symbolizing defeat of the four negative forces—that is, the four *maras* of 1) death, 2) the five aggregates, 3) mental afflictions, that is, disturbing attitudes and negative emotions, and 4) interfering forces.

The other 992 hands all come out of two shoulders—one on the left, the other on the right. Serkong Rinpoche once gave us a formula for how they are arranged, so many in the first row, so many in the second row, etc., but I can't remember it. His Holiness once said when he was talking about it, "How can all those arms come out of just one shoulder?!" It is hard to imagine!

An antelope skin is draped over his left shoulder. For us, the skin of a dead animal represents anything but compassion, but here it is reminiscent of a story about an antelope that gave its life to prevent two hunters from harming each other. The hunters were sneaky. Knowing that the antelope was compassionate, they pretended to fight so that it would try to stop them. When the antelope did just that, the hunters snagged it. The idea behind the story is that the animal was so compassionate that it risked its life to prevent others from quarreling.

Do the visualization as clearly as you are able, and you'll gradually develop more clarity on the details. The most important thing is to get a sense of being in the presence of an enlightened one. Some people get so focused on the details that they lose the feeling of being in the presence of the Buddha. This happens when they see meditation and visualization as a technical skill instead of as a method for spiritual opening. Furthermore, some people "compete" with themselves to have better and better visualizations, thinking, "Can I get as good a visualization today as I did yesterday? Am I doing it right?" We must drop all that and focus on opening our hearts and being with Chenrezig.

REFUGE AND BODHICITTA

At this point we visualize Chenrezig in order to take refuge in him as the embodiment of all the Buddhas, Dharma, and Sangha. We can also expand the visualization, imagining him surrounded by all the Buddhas, bodhisattvas, arhats, other holy beings, and the lineage of teachers down to the teacher who introduced us to this practice.

Because we're taking refuge in a Mahayana way, compassion is a key element. Therefore, we visualize ourselves surrounded by all sentient beings and imagine that we're leading them in taking refuge in the Three Jewels. We visualize our mother on our left and our father on our right. It doesn't matter if our parents are still alive or whether they're Buddhist or not. Wanting them to be happy and leading them to take refuge and generate bodhicitta can be very healing for us, especially if we've had a bumpy relationship with our parents.

The people that we don't like, the people that we're afraid of or feel threatened by, and the people whom we feel uneasy around are all in front of us, right between us and Chenrezig. To see Chenrezig, we have to look at all those people whom we would prefer to ignore. We have to look at Osama bin Laden, George Bush, our ex-husband or ex-wife, the guy who dented our car, and the colleague who got the promotion we felt we deserved. We can't leave them out. We're all facing Chenrezig together, showing that we all have a common motivation of wanting happiness and wanting to be free of suffering. This reminds us that even the people we don't like want to be happy. They're not any less worthy of happiness than anyone else. It also reminds us that to see Chenrezig we have to break through all of our prejudices for and against other people. If we continue to get angry at others, blaming them for our suffering, we're preventing ourselves from connecting with Chenrezig, who is the manifestation of compassion. There's no way to see the Buddha when our minds are overcome by negative emotions and when we believe all the nasty thoughts we have about others. How are we going to "see" emptiness and bodhicitta—which are the Buddha—if our mind is filled with rubbish? Working out our convoluted and confused relationships with these people is an essential part of our spiritual practice. So, don't ignore everyone you don't like and think, "I just want to have a vision of Chenrezig and think about holy beings."

Surrounding us are all sentient beings as far as the eye can see and even beyond that. Think of them all in human form because we will lead them in taking refuge, and it would be hard to lead squirrels and chipmunks in generating the feeling of refuge. Although it's said to imagine we're surrounded by all sentient beings, in actual fact we are always surrounded by sentient beings as far as space exists. So this part is not so much creating a visualization as tuning into what actually is. Similarly, visualizing Chenrezig isn't really a visualization as much as it is tuning into the fact that enlightened beings are around us all the time. We just can't "see" them because of our obscurations.

The Indian sage Asanga meditated for years to have a vision of Maitreya but was unable to. He quit his retreat and walked to town. En route he met a dog with maggots crawling around an injury. With compassion for both the dog and the maggots, he tried to extract the maggots gently with his tongue and place them on his own flesh. It was at that moment that Maitreya appeared to him. Maitreya had been with Asanga during his entire retreat, but Asanga could not see him until he had overcome his self-centeredness. It's the same thing with us: There are Buddhas and bodhisattvas all around because a Buddha's mind perceives all phenomena and permeates everywhere. Doing the visualization reminds us of that and helps us purify our obscurations.

When we take refuge, we say, *"I take refuge until I am enlightened in the Buddha, the Dharma, and the Sangha."* Does that mean that after we're enlightened we don't take refuge? What do you think? Don't we become the three objects of refuge when we're enlightened?

"By the positive potential I create by practicing generosity and the other far-reaching attitudes..."—that is, the perfections of ethical discipline, patience, joyous effort, meditative stabilization, and wisdom—*"may I attain Buddhahood in order to benefit all sentient beings."* With refuge, we know what direction we're going in our practice and upon whom we're relying as guides. By generating bodhicitta, our motivation is clear, and we know why we're going in that direction. It can be very helpful to spend some time contemplating the meaning of this verse so that you feel a strong connection with the Three Jewels and a strong wish to benefit all sentient beings by working for enlightenment. The value of the rest of your practice depends on that motivation.

Our motivation will determine whether what we do in the rest of the session is Dharma or not Dharma. If we do the practice with the wish for enlightenment, it results in enlightenment. It creates the cause for enlightenment. If we do the practice with the wish for liberation, it creates the cause for liberation. If we do the same practice with the wish for a good future rebirth, our efforts will ripen in that way. If we do the practice so that we can feel better now, we will, indeed, feel better, but we won't get any of the other results. The type of result we will experience depends on the motivation with which we create the cause.

There are stories of people who do deity practices of Highest Yoga

Tantra being reborn as spirits. This is due to their having worldly motivations. Even though the meditation method they practice is profound, their motivation is not—for example, they may seek clairvoyant powers so they will feel powerful and others will respect them—and therefore their practice does not bring good results. It is the quality of our motivation that makes something a Dharma practice. Otherwise, we may spend a lot of time visualizing and chanting, but we won't become a kinder or wiser person. To ensure we generate a good motivation, we recite the refuge and bodhicitta verse three times at the beginning of each meditation session. Hopefully we'll pay attention during at least one of those three recitations and cultivate a bodhicitta motivation. Even if we lack spontaneous, effortless bodhicitta, cultivating bodhicitta deliberately and with effort is extraordinarily meaningful.

THE FOUR IMMEASURABLES

To reinforce our bodhicitta motivation, we now meditate on the four immeasurables. Each of the four immeasurables has four parts, or steps, and each step has a slightly different flavor that leads our mind progressively into different states. With each of the four immeasurables, go through the four parts and generate the corresponding feelings. It is very helpful to go through each step slowly, thinking of specific people or situations and taking examples from your own life. Your mind is transformed into a relaxed and open state by doing this meditation.

The first immeasurable is equanimity. The first part is a wish. When we say, *"How wonderful it would be if all sentient beings were to abide in equanimity, free of bias, attachment, and anger,"* we wish for ourselves and all others to abide in that way. The second part, *"May they abide in this way,"* is an aspiration. The third one, *"I shall cause them to abide in this way,"* is a commitment to action on our part. The fourth one, *"Guru Chenrezig, please inspire me to be able to do so,"* is calling out to Chenrezig, requesting his inspiration so that we will have the patience and courage to work continuously to help sentient beings be free of bias, attachment, and anger and to abide in equanimity. Requesting Chenrezig in this way helps us to feel supported in our efforts; we know others have trained their mind and are now capable of doing what we seek to do.

The second immeasurable is love. *"How wonderful it would be if all sentient beings had happiness and its causes."* We meditate on that wish for a while and then go on to, *"May they have these,"* and generate that aspiration. Here, we're not just thinking, "How wonderful if everyone were happy." It's stronger: "May they have happiness. I really want them to have this." Generate that feeling and then go on to the third part and think, *"I shall cause them to have these."* In this part we're getting involved, we're committed. In the fourth part we say, *"Guru Chenrezig, please inspire me to be able to do so."* We seek the aid and inspiration of the Buddhas and bodhisattvas to help us work for the happiness of sentient beings. We can also rely on our own Buddha-nature to inspire and invigorate our practice. Here, feel that your intention is stronger and that you have the courage to work for the happiness of all beings joyfully, without becoming exhausted or discouraged.

The third immeasurable is compassion, wishing sentient beings to be free from suffering. Go through the same four steps when meditating on this—wish, aspiration, commitment, and requesting inspiration.

The fourth immeasurable is joy, wanting sentient beings never to be separated from happiness. Here happiness includes (1) temporal happiness, which is the happiness that exists as long as we're in samsara, and (2) definitive happiness, which is liberation and enlightenment. Fortunate rebirths are considered to be temporal happiness because we enjoy them while in cyclic existence. Liberation and enlightenment are the cessation of suffering and are, therefore, definitive happiness and bliss; they are beyond the vacillations of cyclic existence.

The key word in the four immeasurables is *all. All* sentient beings. "All" is a short word with great meaning. We don't simply think, "May my friends, relatives, and everyone who loves me have happiness and its causes." Even animals want that. We are human beings, so we try to extend the limits of our love beyond those of an animal and so we practice thinking, "May the person who cut me off on the highway have happiness and its causes. May that doctor who gave me the wrong prescription have happiness and its causes. May the person who hung up on me, the person who complained about me at work, my friend who won't speak to me, my cousin who doesn't invite me to her parties— may all these people have happiness and its causes."

When our compassion becomes strong, we will be able to think and feel, "May Timothy McVeigh (the man responsible for the Oklahoma City bombing) and Saddam Hussein have happiness and its causes and be free from suffering and its causes. May George W. Bush and Bill Clinton have happiness and its causes and be free from suffering and its causes." We must try gradually to extend the scope of our equanimity, love, compassion, and joy, spreading them out to *all* sentient beings, not excluding even one. *All!*

If our heart shuts down when thinking of one sentient being and we can't bring ourselves to include them in "all," we should stop and observe what's happening in our heart/mind. With compassion for ourselves, we ask, "What in me is resistant to this? Am I hurt? Angry?" When we become aware of what we're feeling, then we apply Dharma antidotes, for example remembering that this person hasn't always been who they are now. In our past life, he was our best friend or someone who rescued us from danger. Thinking like this, we begin to see him as kind in that way, and our heart can open and wish him well.

It's important to remember that "all sentient beings" includes us as well. We are part of "all." Sometimes we forget to include ourselves in the scope of our equanimity, love, compassion, and joy, and in the end that leaves us feeling dry and isolated. While we want to overcome the wish for only our own happiness, let's not go to the extreme of wishing for everyone's happiness except our own.

THE SPECIAL ALTRUISTIC INTENTION

The verse on the special altruistic intention reinforces our bodhicitta motivation and makes us closer to Chenrezig. *"Especially for the sake of all mother sentient beings"* reminds us that all sentient beings have been our kind mothers in the past. *"I must quickly and more quickly…"* This can be interpreted in two ways. In the first interpretation, "quickly" means by the Sutrayana path and "more quickly" means by the Vajrayana path. In the second interpretation, "quickly" means by the three lower tantric paths and "more quickly" means by the Highest Yoga Tantra path. In this case, because Chenrezig is a lower tantric practice (*Kriya Tantra*), we use the first interpretation.

Then we say, "*...in this very life, attain the precious state of complete and perfect enlightenment.*" My teachers have advised us to aspire for enlightenment in this lifetime but not to expect to attain it. Aspiring to attain enlightenment quickly is important, because if we don't aspire to that, we definitely won't attain it. Nevertheless, we should avoid expecting to instantly attain everything we aspire to and abandon the "quick-fix mind" that expects to get enlightened immediately. That mind is a set-up for disappointment. His Holiness the Dalai Lama says our impatience and wish for dramatic results is one of the biggest problems we Westerners face in Dharma practice.

We aim to become a Buddha in the long run. What else are we going to do? We've already been born in each of the six realms countless times in the past. In our infinite previous lives, we have done everything and have experienced every pleasure and suffering in cyclic existence. There's absolutely nothing new or exciting to do in cyclic existence. In fact, samsara is actually quite boring as well as totally senseless. If we want to do something really new and experience something we've never experienced before, let's practice the path to enlightenment. We've had many romantic relationships in our beginningless infinite lifetimes; they are nothing new. But we've never had pure love that is completely free from attachment, a kind of love that spreads to each and every sentient being and doesn't vacillate according to how sentient beings treat us. Let's try and develop such a quality—that's really doing something interesting, new, and exciting, not to mention highly meaningful. Attaining full enlightenment is an incredibly valuable, useful thing to do in life.

Because we want to become a Buddha, we practice the Guru Chenrezig yoga. We say "Guru Chenrezig" here to make this a practice of guru yoga. In other words, we see Chenrezig as the nature of the ulti-mate guru, which is the transcendental wisdom of bliss and emptiness. This wisdom manifests in various forms, such as Chenrezig and the spiritual master who gave us the empowerment into this practice. While we can think of this wisdom appearing as each of our spiritual masters, we especially think of the teacher who gave us the initiation as the embodiment of the transcendental wisdom of bliss and emptiness. It can be very inspiring to think, "My teacher is appearing in the form of Chenrezig," as if he or she were there, looking after us as we practice. If we have much love, respect, and gratitude for our teacher, thinking that he or she is Chenrezig makes Chenrezig come alive for us.

The transcendental bliss and emptiness manifest in many different aspects—Chenrezig, Tara, Manjushri, Shakyamuni Buddha, and so forth—according to the needs of sentient beings. This wisdom—the ultimate guru, the blissful omniscient minds of all the Buddhas—can also manifest as a blanket, a dog, our spiritual teacher, our best friend, and even as our worst enemy. The wisdom of all the Buddhas can man-ifest in whatever aspect is needed to lead us along the path at any par-ticular moment.

Saying "Guru Chenrezig" doesn't mean we should focus on the per-sonality of our spiritual teacher and think, "Wow! That person is Chen-rezig. I want his autograph!" This is a Hollywood mentality that misses the point of creating a good relationship with a spiritual mentor. Becoming infatuated with the personality of our teacher creates blocks in our practice. Instead of putting the teachings into practice and trans-forming our minds, we worship external people, thinking they will bless us and make us into Buddhas. With this thought, we don't exert effort in our practice. If we become attached to the personality of our teacher, thinking that person is inherently holy and special, then when our teacher dies, we feel like we've lost our refuge. I saw this happen when Lama Yeshe passed away. Some people didn't understand who Lama really was and thus lost their inspiration to practice the Dharma when Lama's physical body and personality were no longer present.

In addition, if we become infatuated with our teachers, we may forget that their purpose is to guide us to enlightenment. Instead, we may expect them to fulfill our emotional needs. As a result, we feel rejected when our teachers are busy and don't have time to see us. We become jealous of other disciples who have more of our teachers' attention, and we start seeking our teachers' approval just as young children seek their parents' approval to feel good about themselves. Such emotional machinations get us tangled up, so that we forget the actual purpose of having a spiritual mentor. While a very deep bond may exist between spiritual mentor and disciple, we must realize that our teachers are not our personal property. They work for all sentient beings; they belong to the universe.

2. *Purifying Negativities and Accumulating Positive Potential*

The Seven-Limb Prayer

THE THREE SECTIONS of refuge and bodhicitta, the four immeasurables, and the special altruistic intention are designed to help us fine-tune and strengthen our motivation. Then, we go on to the seven-limb prayer to purify and accumulate positive potential, or merit, as it is often translated.

Doing the self-generation practice is similar to dying and being reborn. In the self-generation, we meditate on emptiness and let go of our attachment to the ego of this life and our grasping at a real self. In that way, meditating on emptiness is like dying, because we can no longer hold on to the idea, "This is who I am. This is what I like and what I don't like." Our conception of who we are is severely challenged and is relinquished. When we do the self-generation, we arise as Chenrezig, which is similar to being reborn as Chenrezig instead of being reborn in samsara. Instead of coming into the world with the wail of a newborn child, we arise with the thoughts of love and compassion.

Before ordinary beings like us die and take rebirth, it's good if we purify our negative karma and accumulate positive potential in order to prepare for death. In this way, we die without fear and have a wealth of goodness that supports us as we traverse the intermediate state and enter our next life. Likewise in the sadhana, before we meditate on emptiness and generate ourselves as Chenrezig, we perform purification and accumulation practices.

Purification and accumulation of positive potential are excellent practices to do when our mind feels stale or crusty, or when we feel stuck in our lives or in our Dharma practice. If we're bored and don't have any feeling when we meditate, it often indicates the need to do more purification and accumulation of positive potential. That's why in the Tibetan tradition there are practices such as 100,000 prostrations, 100,000 mandala offerings, and 100,000 Vajrasattva mantras. The seven-limb prayer is an excellent method to purify and accumulate positive potential. There are long and short versions of it. The short version is in this sadhana, but a longer version taken from *The King of Prayers* is in the Nyung Nä sadhana. The seven limbs are:

1. Prostrations
2. Offering
3. Revealing negativities
4. Rejoicing
5. Asking the Buddhas to remain
6. Requesting the Buddhas and our teachers to teach us
7. Dedication of positive potential.

1. Prostrations

"Reverently I prostrate with my body, speech, and mind." The first of the seven limbs is prostrations, which are physical, verbal, and mental. We can stand and do physical prostrations if we wish, but putting our palms together at our heart is sufficient. Saying the above line is verbal prostration. Visualizing ourselves surrounded by all sentient beings who are also bowing and showing homage and generating respect in our mind constitute mental prostration. Prostrations are particularly good for purifying pride because we have our nose on the ground. We may initially feel uncomfortable humbling ourselves, but later we recognize what a relief it is to let go of having to "be someone." Prostrations help us to generate respect for others' good qualities. The more we can see and respect others' good qualities, the more we can open to and develop those good qualities in ourselves.

2. Offering

"And present clouds of every type of offering, actual and mentally trans-formed." The second limb is offering. Actual offerings are the ones on the altar. Mentally transformed offerings are the ones we visualize. We imagine clouds of offerings of very beautiful things, especially things that we like and are attached to. Make them bigger, of better quality, and more glittering. These offerings don't break, they don't decay. They're made of light, and we offer them all to Chenrezig. "Clouds of offerings" doesn't mean we visualize clouds with offerings on them; it means that the sky is filled with offerings.

If your mind is obsessing with desire for something, imagine that, make it more wonderful in your mind, and then offer it to Chenrezig. Think that Chenrezig is delighted and experiences bliss, and you, too, feel good about making the offering. You can do this with people that you're attached to as well—imagine them and then mentally offer them to Chenrezig, thinking that they are now under Chenrezig's care and guidance. This doesn't mean we don't love them; we do still, but we realize that they're better off under Chenrezig's guidance than under our jealous and possessive attachment. By offering them to Chenrezig we release our clinging so that when we relate to them in the future, we are more relaxed.

Offering purifies miserliness and creates delight in giving. We feel good about giving, and this is essential for practice because the path and the result are all about giving. No one ever heard of a stingy Buddha or a bodhisattva who couldn't share her time with others.

3. Revealing Negativities

"I confess all of my negative actions accumulated since beginningless time." The third limb is revealing our negativities, also called confession. The Tibetan word for confession is *shak*, which means "to split open" or "to reveal." Confessing helps us stop denying our mistakes and problems. We admit that not all our actions have been kind and wise; we acknowl-

edge that we have harmed others and made mistakes both intentional-
ly and unintentionally. In this limb, we're willing to admit our mistakes,
to let go of attachment to our reputation, to stop putting up a good
defense, and to give up rationalizing our actions so that we look good
or innocent. Here, we're letting go of all that, acknowledging to ourselves and to Chenrezig that we've made mistakes. Doing this can bring
a tremendous sense of relief inside of us, because we no longer have to
justify things we don't feel good about doing to ourselves or to others.

The third limb includes the four opponent powers:

1. Generating regret, not guilt, when acknowledging our mistakes
2. Restoring the relationship by taking refuge and generating bodhicitta
3. Promising to avoid doing that action again in the future, at least
   for a period of time that we can reasonably keep
4. Engaging in remedial action, such as mantra recitation, reciting
   the names of Buddhas, doing volunteer work in the community,
   making material offerings or offering service to monasteries,
   Dharma centers, the poor, and those who are ill.

4. Rejoicing

"And rejoice in the virtues of all holy and ordinary beings." The fourth limb
is rejoicing. Holy beings are those on the path of seeing and above;
these are beings who have perceived reality—the emptiness of inherent existence—directly. Ordinary beings are all other sentient beings,
including ourselves. Here we rejoice in everyone's positive potential
and goodness.

Rejoicing is an antidote to being jealous of others' good qualities,
abilities, and virtue. It's also an excellent antidote for depression. Rather
than thinking about how awful the world is, how terrible we are, how
hopeless the world seems, we make our mind happy by thinking of all
the positive qualities that we and others have and all the beneficial
actions we and others have done. Rejoicing creates great positive poten-

tial (merit) and makes our mind happy and optimistic. It also enables us to have a more realistic view of the world by seeing the goodness of living beings, not just their suffering and defilements.

5. Asking the Buddhas to Remain

"Please remain until cyclic existence ends." The fifth limb is asking the Buddhas and our spiritual teachers to live long and guide us until our own and all others' cyclic existence ends. This purifies negativities created in relation to our spiritual mentors and helps us to appreciate the presence of holy beings in our lives. Here, we imagine offering a double dorje, symbolizing long life, to Chenrezig. This symbol of long life is often seen in front of the teacher's seat in a temple.

6. Requesting Teachings

"And turn the wheel of Dharma for sentient beings." The sixth limb is asking our teachers and the Buddhas and bodhisattvas to teach us. This helps us not to take our teachers for granted and generates within us the wish to receive teachings in the future. It also purifies negativities that we've generated in relation to our teachers or the Buddhas and bodhisattvas.

Asking our spiritual mentors to teach and to live long is very important. In our busy lives it is easy to forget how precious they are, the important function they play in our lives, and their kindness in guiding us on the path. When we stop feeling these, we lose inspiration to practice and become careless in our actions. But when these are prominent in our mind, the energy to make use of our precious human life flows naturally.

7. Dedication of Positive Potential

"I dedicate all the virtues of myself and others to the great enlightenment." The seventh limb is dedication. The "great enlightenment" refers to

the full enlightenment of a Buddha. We dedicate all our own and others' virtues; and doing this brings us joy. When we dedicate for our own and others' enlightenment, this includes dedicating to have all the circumstances conducive to practice while we're still in cyclic existence. This limb protects our virtue from being hampered or destroyed by anger or wrong views.

One time a man came to me for meditation instructions and at the end of the session I led him in dedicating the positive potential. He looked at me with dismay and said, "But I have so little merit, I don't want to dedicate it to others." I explained to him that positive potential isn't like money—when we spend it we no longer have it—but that it expands the more we share it with others.

MANDALA OFFERING

Next, we do the mandala offering, which is actually included in the limb of offering. When offering a mandala, we imagine offering the entire universe. Here, we imagine the universe according to the ancient Indian cosmology of a world that's flat, with Mount Meru at the center, four continents, eight subcontinents, and so forth. The masters encourage us to visualize it in detail, but personally speaking, if it's a choice between imagining the details of the wish-fulfilling jewel, one of the objects of offering in the mandala, and having the feeling of offering the world and everything beautiful in it, I think the latter is more important.

Instead of offering the world and all that's in it to our own egos, which is what we usually do, we offer it to the Buddhas and bodhisattvas in appreciation for their guidance and teachings. Offering the mandala creates a tremendous sense of abundance. We offer all the beauty, riches, and success of the world without any attachment or expectation. Some people offer the mandala 100,000 times, again and again imagining beautiful things and offering them to the Three Jewels. This creates a feeling of richness inside of us: "I offer the world without any sense of loss on my part, and my doing this creates so much joy in the mind of all Buddhas." We take so much delight in giving, which opens our heart and frees us from the constriction and fear caused by miserliness.

Here the mandala offering has two verses. In the first verse we offer the outer mandala, the physical universe and everything beautiful in it. Instead of thinking of the universe in an ordinary way, we imagine it as a pure land, a Buddha-land where everything is lovely and all beings are peaceful. In this place, we have all the conditions conducive for practicing the Dharma. We offer the mandala with the aspiration, "May everyone enjoy this pure land. May everyone be happy and be able to practice with good conditions."

The second verse is offering the inner mandala. Here we offer things connected with sentient beings' mindstreams, specifically our body. In other words, we imagine our body itself becoming the mandala, and then we offer it. The inside of our body is rather disgusting, so we don't offer our ordinary kidneys and liver. Instead, we transform the parts of our body into beautiful objects and offer those. This helps our mind to stop being attached to this meat-and-blood body that is really not so gorgeous. Instead, we imagine transforming our body into the universe and offering it to the Three Jewels. By doing so, we create positive potential, which is much more useful to us when we die than this body is. When we die, this body will not come with us, but our positive potential will. This meditation helps us make good use of our body while we have it.

In this visualization, our skin transforms into the golden ground; our intestines become the circles of mountains; and our blood becomes the rivers and oceans. Our torso becomes Mount Meru; our hands and feet transform into the four continents; our upper and lower arms and our calves and thighs become the eight subcontinents; our eyes are the sun and moon; our ears become the victory banner and parasol; and our internal organs transform into spectacular offerings that fill the entire sky. Meditating in this way is an excellent antidote to attachment to our body. If you're afraid of dying and losing your body, practice this visualization a lot. If your body is aging and you're attached to it being young and attractive, practicing this visualization will help you to be content with your body and to accept the aging process gracefully. If we're conceited because our body is young or athletic, practicing this meditation eliminates this arrogance. It's a very freeing meditation.

Next, we offer objects of attachment, aversion, and ignorance—friends, enemies and strangers, our body, wealth, and enjoyments. "Enjoyments" means the things we use and enjoy, for example, computers, bank accounts, skis, summer homes, artwork, jewelry, CDs, tattoos and body piercings, digital equipment, cars, and so forth. Whatever we enjoy, and thus tend to cling to as "mine," we offer all of it.

"I offer these without any sense of loss" has great meaning. So often we are afraid to give; the thought arises, "If I give this, I won't have it," and that brings fear into our hearts. Suffering from this kind of fear, some people in rich countries are stingy. Their closets, drawers, and basement are filled with things—many of which they've forgotten they even have—yet they cannot give them to others. Thoughts such as "I may need this in five years" fill their minds, and even though they probably won't ever use the object, they are unable to give it to someone who could use it now. What great mental suffering this is! If you've traveled in Third World countries, you know that many poor people are much more generous than wealthy people in rich countries. We have to get over the concept that generosity is the cause of poverty and realize that, karmically, giving brings wealth in the future and great joy in the mind right now.

"Please accept them with pleasure and inspire me and others to be free from the three poisonous attitudes," of ignorance, anger, and attachment. "IDAM GURU RATNA MANDALAKAM NIRYATAYAMI" means "I offer this precious jeweled mandala to my spiritual teacher." This, too, helps us to purify miserliness and attachment and to create a lot of positive potential.

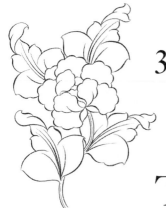

3 *Request Prayer*

THE REQUEST PRAYER to Chenrezig fills our heart with inspiration when we say it with sincerity. An American nun set the English translation of the verses to the melody that we sing. From the words, it may sound as if we're requesting Chenrezig to please do this and that for us. However, what we're actually doing is projecting Chenrezig outside of ourselves—projecting our own potential and good qualities outside of ourselves—and then making requests to our own Buddha-nature, our own potential. We also request the beings who are Chenrezig, who have spiritual realizations that we ordinary beings don't have. This invigorates us to practice so we may become Buddhas and possess the same wisdom, compassion, and skillful means that Chenrezig has.

We ask Chenrezig, who embodies our own Buddha-nature in its completely purified and endowed form, to cleanse our minds from beginningless defilements and to grant us realizations of the path to enlightenment. The beings who are already Chenrezig can't actually do that, but some kind of dependent arising process occurs when we are with holy beings or in holy places. Something affects our mind. Many people have told me that even though they have never met His Holiness the Dalai Lama before, they start to cry when he walks into the auditorium, and they have no idea why. Sometimes people have significant spiritual experiences when they meditate in Bodhgaya, India, the place where the Buddha attained enlightenment. Our mind opens up there, and we may have deep experiences of teachings that before were mere words to us. The more openness and faith that we have in the Buddhas' qualities and the more we recite this request prayer, the more our own minds will open to that kind of inspiration or blessing.

That inspiration or opening is a dependent arising. I can't exactly explain how it works, but we come to understand it from experience as we practice. I asked His Holiness the Dalai Lama about receiving inspiration or blessing, and he responded that it depends on the mind of the person requesting and the mind of the beings who are requested. He said that someone might pray to the president of the country, but questioned, "Does the president have the ability to grant you blessings? Can the president, from his or her side, inspire or transform your mind?" Someone like a president doesn't have the ability to affect us spiritually because he or she is confused and is trapped in cyclic existence just as we are. But, when we request the Buddhas or highly realized spiritual masters, they can help us spiritually. For example, it is said that someone without realizations can speak about the Dharma for hours but no one gets inspired, whereas someone with realizations can say a few words and the audience benefits greatly and is inspired to practice. Even if someone practices and has just small experiences of the Dharma, her words carry more force that those of someone who only knows the teachings intellectually or academically.

Something happens due to the power of the mind. So when we make requests to beings such as Chenrezig, who are free from samsara, some kind of energy can be transmitted. I don't know if this can be explained through scientific tools, but I did read that studies have shown that people for whom others pray recover more swiftly from surgery and injuries than others. There are many things that science can't explain. Maybe one day scientists will analyze the brains of nuns and monks and find the chemical of Chenrezig's special blessing! Then someone could patent it and make it into a pill! I'm joking!

"O Arya Compassionate-Eyed One." "Arya" means someone who has attained the path of seeing or above. Chenrezig is completely enlightened. As the Compassionate-Eyed One, he looks at everyone with compassion, not with scorn or derision, condescension or blame, but

with compassion. Chenrezig is a good example for us. He reminds us of how to look at our family members, colleagues, and all beings.

"Who is the treasure of compassion." He has an overabundance of compassion, like a credit card with no limit. *"I request you, please listen to me."* What we're really saying is, "I'm listening to you, Chenrezig." Actually, Chenrezig is paying attention to us all the time, but we usually do not pay attention to Chenrezig or the other Buddhas and bodhisattvas. Here, we trick ourselves by saying, "Please listen to me," as if the Buddhas have to take time off from their golf game to pay attention to us. But we're really saying that we're taking time off from our hectic work day, filled with television, traffic, and email, to pay attention to Chenrezig.

"Please guide myself, mothers, and fathers in all six realms to be freed quickly." This includes all hell beings, hungry ghosts, animals, humans, gods, and demi-gods. We don't want happiness just for ourselves, but for each and every living being. *"From the great ocean of samsara."* We are drowning in the ocean of ignorance and *dukkha*—all the unsatisfactory conditions involved with being in cyclic existence. How does Chenrezig free us? Not by throwing us a life raft; not by calling in the Navy SEALs with their helicopters; but by giving us teachings. When we receive teachings and practice them, we liberate ourselves.

"I request that the vast and profound peerless awakening mind may grow." The peerless awakening mind is bodhicitta. The vast bodhicitta is compassion, the method side of the path. The profound bodhicitta is the wisdom realizing emptiness, the wisdom side of the path. We request Chenrezig to assist us and others in generating these two bodhicittas, the altruistic intention or conventional bodhicitta and the wisdom directly realizing emptiness or ultimate bodhicitta, because those minds will liberate us. We request these not only for ourselves, but for everyone. Think about it. "May Adolph Hitler, Joseph Stalin, Mao Tsetung, and Osama bin Laden generate the conventional and ultimate bodhicittas. May Timothy McVeigh generate the two bodhicittas." That's much more beneficial than wanting to watch his execution on closed circuit TV. "May George W. Bush, Ariel Sharon, and Yassar

Arafat have wisdom and compassion." Think how different our world would be if all our leaders had the vast and profound bodhicittas. Thinking like this is applying the Dharma to the events happening around us.

"With the tear of your great compassion, please cleanse all karmas and delusions." Delusions refer to our disturbing attitudes and negative emotions, all 84,000 afflictions. Karmas are the contaminated actions that we've engaged in under their influence. We are stating our aspiration to lay these aside and to cleanse them from our mindstream so that they no longer bind us in cyclic existence.

"Please lead with your hand of compassion me and migrators to fields of bliss." What a beautiful image! A hand of compassion! Think of a thousand hands of compassion reaching out to us, a thousand hands that we can grab onto, that will lead us to safety beyond afflictions, their seeds, and their imprints. What we really grab onto is the teachings. That is, we generate the meaning of the teachings in our own minds. By Chenrezig's hand of compassion and by our holding the teachings in our hearts, may we and all others be reborn in fields of bliss.

We sentient beings are called migrators because we migrate from one unsatisfactory rebirth to another. Going to Chenrezig's field of bliss, the pure land of Sukhavati, may sound like a physical occurrence with Chenrezig stretching out his hand and pulling us up to Sukhavati. However, it's not like that. Rather, by receiving Dharma teachings and integrating them into our own hearts and minds, we become liberated. Sukhavati arises inside us; it's a mental state. Sukhavati isn't two clouds up and one cloud to the left. We can't go there by airplane, magic carpet, or by an inherently existent Chenrezig holding our hand.

Sukhavati is spoken of as a physical place, where beings are born inside lotus buds and where even the sound of wind blowing through the trees teaches them the Dharma. But we shouldn't see it as an external place separate from and unrelated to the mind. High-level bodhisattvas can make their internal, pure mental states manifest as external places for the benefit of sentient beings. But for us to go to those places, we need to have developed certain internal mental states ourselves.

"Please, Amitabha and Chenrezig, in all my lives be virtuous friends."
Amitabha Buddha is the head of Sukhavati. We request him and his
assistant, Chenrezig, to manifest as our spiritual mentors in all of our
lives. It's so important to aspire, "In all of our lives, may we be guided
by perfectly qualified Mahayana and Vajrayana teachers." This aspiration steers our mind so that we will meet qualified spiritual mentors in
all our future lives. This is essential because if we meet teachers of
wrong paths, we will learn incorrect teachings, and however much we
may practice them, we will not attain valid spiritual realizations. For
example, if the cook isn't qualified and doesn't know what he's doing,
all the food he prepares tastes bad, and we end up getting sick instead
of having a good meal.

It's important to make prayers to meet fully qualified teachers who
are manifestations of Buddhas and bodhisattvas. We must aspire not
only to meet such teachers but also to have good relationships with
them, to be open to the teachings they give, and to be able to follow
their instruction properly. We may meet qualified teachers, but if our
mind is closed, they can't help us. So, we have to aspire to be qualified
disciples: to have an open mind, to have a healthy relationship with
our teachers, to listen attentively, and to put into practice what they
teach us.

In all our lives, from now until enlightenment, may Amitabha and
Chenrezig be our spiritual mentors and guide us. And may they *"Show
well the undeceptive pure path and quickly place us in Buddha's state."* The
undeceptive pure path is the path of the wisdom realizing the emptiness of inherent existence and the bodhicitta aspiring to become a Buddha in order to benefit all sentient beings. May we always hear
teachings on the correct view of emptiness. It's extremely important to
pray for that, because if we don't hear accurate teachings on the correct
view, we can meditate for eons on what we think is the correct view of
emptiness but won't directly realize the emptiness of inherent existence.
In addition, if we don't properly understand what meditation is, we
may do what we think is meditation, but instead our mind may become
spaced out, and we may be reborn as an animal in the next life. So, we

want to make sure to receive undeceptive pure teachings on the undeceptive pure path. Through receiving those teachings and practicing them well, may we attain enlightenment; that is, may we be placed in Buddha's state.

This prayer to Avalokiteshvara is a way for us to express our highest and most deeply felt aspirations in the presence of the Buddhas and bodhisattvas. Do this prayer with a lot of feeling, from the depth of your heart. I remember sometimes when we chanted this request during Nyung Nä, we would start crying from the force of our faith and pure aspiration.

At this point you may insert "A Lamentation Requesting Blessings from the Great Compassionate One" and recite that while contemplating its meaning. Or you may recite it separately from the sadhana. If recited before you begin the sadhana, you may be filled with inspiration to do the Chenrezig practice and that will make your concentration stronger.

4 *The Eight Verses of Thought Transformation*

The *Eight Verses of Thought Transformation* is not part of the Nyung Nä sadhana. It's a separate text, but Lama Zopa Rinpoche inserted it here because practicing thought training enables us to become Chenrezig. These verses tell us how Chenrezig views life, what Chenrezig thinks and feels. Thought training is about the two bodhicittas, which are Chenrezig's nature. The more we meditate on thought training, the closer we come to Chenrezig; the more we become like Chenrezig.

After reciting each verse, we may say OM MANI PADME HUM a few times, imagining light coming from Chenrezig into us. The light purifies our internal obstacles—the tangled emotions that prevent us from actualizing the meaning of that verse. The light also inspires our mind to develop the receptivity, compassion, and love to actualize it. Or, if we prefer, we can meditate silently after saying each verse, contemplating its meaning and applying it to situations in our life. Doing this is extremely effective for bringing home to us the purpose of the verses. These verses are to be practiced, not just recited or prayed.

1. With the thought of attaining enlightenment
    For the welfare of all beings,
    Who are more precious than a wish-fulfilling jewel,
    I will constantly practice holding them dear.

"With the thought of attaining enlightenment for the welfare of all beings" refers to bodhicitta, wanting to attain enlightenment to benefit all beings. *"Who are more precious than a wish-fulfilling jewel"* shows the value of sentient beings. A wish-fulfilling jewel in ancient Indian culture is a mythic gem that could grant whatever one wished for. Here, sentient beings are more precious than this jewel because, through caring for sentient beings, we attain enlightenment. An ordinary wish-fulfilling jewel could bring fame, wealth, power, love, family, beauty, athletic ability, and so forth. But those things don't provide ultimate happiness. They fade with time, and even while we have them, they bring a lot of new problems. Enlightenment, on the other hand, doesn't have such drawbacks.

Often we see other sentient beings as hassles: "This mosquito is disturbing me. Those politicians are corrupt. Why can't my colleagues do their work correctly?" and so on. But when we see sentient beings as being more precious than a wish-fulfilling jewel, our perspective completely changes. For example, when we look at a fly buzzing around, we train ourselves to think, "My enlightenment depends on that fly." This isn't fanciful thinking because, in fact, our enlightenment *does* depend on that fly. If that fly isn't included in our bodhicitta, then we don't have bodhicitta, and we won't receive the wonderful results of generating bodhicitta—the tremendous purification and creation of positive potential. Imagine training your mind so that when you look at every single living being, you think, "My enlightenment depends on that being. The drunk who just got on the bus—my enlightenment depends on him. The soldier in Iraq—my enlightenment depends on him. My brothers and sisters, the teller at the bank, the janitor at my workplace, the president of the United States, the suicide bombers in the Middle East, the slug in my garden, my eighth-grade boyfriend, the babysitter when I was a kid—my enlightenment depends on each of them." All sentient beings are actually that precious to us.

Furthermore, the fact that we're even alive and have the possibility to practice the Dharma is due to the kindness of each and every sentient being. Everything we use and enjoy—clothes, food, teachings—

is created by or dependent on sentient beings. So many people are involved in the growing, transporting, packaging, selling, and preparation of the ingredients in even one meal that we eat. The forests we love to stroll in exist due to the ecosystem that consists of zillions of sentient beings. We are unimaginably indebted to sentient beings. When we think about it deeply, something inside of us shakes. We stop feeling like isolated individuals who are entitled to better treatment. We realize how incredibly fortunate we are; we open to the fact that we've been the recipient of unbelievable kindness throughout our entire life.

Because of this, *"I will constantly practice holding them dear."* Instead of being jealous of others who are more skilled in a particular area than we are, instead of competing with them because we want to be better than them, instead of being arrogant because we're more accomplished than them, instead of being attached to them and drawing them into our trips, instead of being angry at them and causing them lots of problems, instead of being spiteful and criticizing them behind their backs, instead of being rebellious and uncooperative, we're going to practice holding them dear. We've got our work cut out for us, don't we? But what magnificent results will come now and in the future as we do this work!

At the beginning, our bodhicitta is contrived; that is, we have to put energy into contemplating the kindness of others and the other steps to generate bodhicitta before any feeling for it comes. With uncontrived bodhicitta, whenever we see any sentient being, our spontaneous reaction is one wishing to attain full enlightenment in order to benefit all sentient beings most effectively. Clearly, lots of practice over a long period of time is necessary in order to familiarize our mind with this new reaction to sentient beings.

If we do something to benefit one sentient being, it's that powerful. If we do something to benefit ten sentient beings, it's more powerful. If we do something to benefit all sentient beings, it's super powerful, especially because our wish is to lead them to the highest happiness, enlightenment. Any action we do with bodhicitta makes a strong imprint on our mindstream. It counteracts our self-centeredness and the actions we have done motivated by it. It accumulates potent positive potential because we wish the best for each and every sentient being and we commit ourselves to bringing that about. Because bodhicitta depends on every single sentient being, those sentient beings become more precious to us than a wish-fulfilling jewel. If a wish-fulfilling jewel gets lost, it's not a huge problem, but if we leave one sentient being out of the sphere of our compassion, we lack bodhicitta and our highest spiritual aspirations will be thwarted.

2.   Whenever I am with others
     I will practice seeing myself as the lowest of all,
     And from the very depth of my heart
     I will respectfully hold others as supreme.

It's important to understand this verse properly. It is not a prescription for low self-esteem. Holding ourselves as lowest of all doesn't mean we hate ourselves or think we're worthless. It doesn't mean we don't respect ourselves. It simply means we stop making a big deal out of ourselves or insisting that everything center on what we want.

Generally, when we're with others, who do we care the most about? ME! "I want all the nice things to happen to me. I want to be first in line, I want the most food. I want to be appreciated. I work so hard, and the least that sentient beings can do is thank me for everything I do for them. I want to be acknowledged for my talents, deeds, and achievements. I want to be right. I want people to know how accomplished I am. I want people to love me and approve of me. I want others to listen to me and follow my instructions." Our thoughts center on me, me, me! According to ego—self-grasping ignorance—"I" and "me" are the center of the universe.

When we feel "I am the lowest of all," suddenly there is some space. When we pop the bubble of "I," there's space to see beauty, space to feel connected with others, space to be satisfied. But, when we're preoccupied with "me," we become overly sensitive and react to everything and everyone. Somebody looks at us, and instead of being able to greet them with a smile, we wonder, "What does his look mean? Does he think he's better than me? Does he respect me? Does he appreciate me? Does he love me enough? Does he realize who *I* am?" We are so reactive in every interaction with others: "They don't like women. They don't like men. They don't like Americans. They don't like vegetarians. They're jealous of people who are successful." Whatever we are, they don't like it, we're sure! We become fearful and anxious and think we have to struggle to be acknowledged or fight for our rights whenever we're with others. We project on them all sorts of negative qualities and then hate them for being what we've projected. Self-defeating, isn't it? When that mindset is manifest, we lack the ability to connect with others. People may care for us or respect us, but we can't see it through the screen of our own projections.

Someone might say, "But sometimes people really are nasty to us!" I do prison work, and prison is not a pleasant or a safe place to live. One man told me that he realized soon after he went in that he had two choices: either be understanding of those around him, let things go, and keep a happy mind, or take everything personally, get depressed, and lash out at those around him. There was no third choice. So he chose the first one and made it through his sentence okay.

Another inmate said to me, "As much as you may think fire is water, it's still going to burn you, so trying to change the way you look at things isn't going to help." I replied, "But what if you think a rope is a snake?" He sat up straight. He'd understood.

When we see ourselves as the lowest of all, we drop this self-preoccupation. We open our eyes and realize that the universe is pop-ulated with other living beings, and from the depths of our hearts we respectfully hold them as supreme. We cherish them, instead of think-ing, "Here I am. Everyone should learn from me! Everyone should do things my way because my way is best. They should follow my instruc-tions because I have the best idea." It just means dropping all of that self-centeredness! When we drop that, our minds are so much more peaceful. When we stop interacting with everyone in terms of "Where do I stand in relationship to you and what do you think of me?," we will be able to connect with them. And that's what we all long for, isn't it? None of us likes remaining isolated in our own self-created hell.

That's what "seeing ourselves as the lowest of all" involves. We don't have to be acknowledged. We don't have to be respected. We don't have to be approved of. This doesn't mean we put ourselves in a position to be stomped on. It just means that we drop our self-preoccupation and the ego-based needs to be loved, respected, acknowledged, and appreciated, and the ego-propelled wishes to win, to be right, and to have our way. We're dropping all this. It's so liberating. We can breathe a sigh of relief and finally relax when we let go of the unhealthy focus on "I."

What do we do with our emotional needs? We can't just pretend they don't exist. Mother Teresa told us what she does:

> When I am hungry, give me someone that I can feed.
> And when I am thirsty, give me someone who needs a drink.
> When I'm cold, give me someone to keep warm.
> And when I grieve, give me someone to console.

Along the same line, His Holiness the Dalai Lama recommends compassion as an antidote to low self-esteem. At first I didn't understand why he said this because it seemed to me that when we don't like ourselves, we need to heal that and learn to love ourselves first. Then I realized that cherishing others takes the unhealthy, egocentric emphasis off ourselves, and in so doing, we are healed.

3. In all actions I will examine my mind,
    And the moment a disturbing attitude arises,
    Endangering myself and others,
    I will firmly confront and avert it.

Here we are mindful: "I will be aware of what's going on in my mind— what I'm thinking and feeling—and by extension, I'll be aware of what I'm saying and doing. Every time a negative emotion arises, instead of saying, 'Anger, welcome! You're my friend. You're going to stick up for me so that other people don't take advantage of me,' I'm going to say, 'Anger, you're a thief. You steal my happiness and peace of mind! I'm not going to get involved with you.'"

It's similar with attachment. Attachment comes into the mind, and instead of saying, "Oh, attachment, you're going to make me happy," we recognize, "Attachment, you're a set-up for suffering. I'm not going to listen to your story!" These disturbing emotions endanger us because they make us create negative karma, leading to future suffering. They also make us miserable right now. Are you happy when you're angry? No! Disturbing emotions endanger others because when we speak and act under their influence, we harm others.

When doubt comes into the mind, we often welcome it: "Doubt, come in. I'm so bored. Go ahead and amuse me. Let's be skeptical of this. Let's challenge that. Let's be suspicious of this." This verse recommends that instead of welcoming doubt, we recognize it: "Doubt, you just play around and make my mind a mess! You make my mind race with all sorts of useless thoughts that tangle me up. I'm aware of your shenanigans. Wisdom, come and chase out this demon of doubt!"

This is the meaning of confronting a negative emotion or disturbing attitude. Then we must also avert it, that is, apply the antidote. For attachment, we meditate on impermanence and the ugly aspect of whatever we're attached to. For anger, we meditate on patience and love. For jealousy, we meditate on rejoicing. For doubt, we meditate on the breath to calm our mind and use wisdom to dispel doubts. Verse 3 means, "I'm going to be a doctor to my own mind."

4.   Whenever I meet a person of bad nature
     Who is overwhelmed by negative energy and intense suffering,
     I will hold such a rare one dear,
     As if I had found a precious treasure.

People of bad nature are people who are cross and difficult to get along with, who challenge our authority or grumble about what we do. Of course, those people may not consider themselves bad-natured, but we do, simply because they don't like us or disagree with our ideas (which are always right). They tune us out, don't pay attention to us, and don't cater to our whims. What uncooperative people!

People who are overwhelmed by negative energy are those who have a lot of anger, jealousy, bitterness, or obsessive craving. Sometimes when we're around such people, we can feel the confusion, restlessness, and disturbance in their minds. We want to turn away from them. It may be your father-in-law who criticizes almost everyone, the teenage boys down the street who are so rowdy, or your ex-wife.

People with intense suffering could be those who are injured, deformed, very ill, or grieving a loss. We tend to shun those people because we feel uncomfortable around them. For example, we don't like going into hospitals. Seeing sick people reminds us of our own mortality. When we encounter people who are disfigured or who have severe emotional problems, we shrink away: "I don't want to talk to that person. All they do is complain!" or "I have to wait on them!" or "They smell bad!" We have so many adverse reactions to other sentient beings. The iron gate in our mind slams shut and excludes them.

I noticed this one day while riding the bus in Seattle. A very large and unattractive man sat next to me. He was listening to his CD player with earphones, but he had turned up the volume so loud that the rest of us could still hear the music. He took up most of the bench and I was squished in the corner. Initially, my heart closed to this person. I wished he would sit somewhere else. Noticing my reaction, I tried to look at him differently. Then I saw a sentient being who's trying to be happy by listening to music and relaxing on the bus. He didn't choose to have a body like that. His body was created by his karma. I realized I didn't have to shut my heart toward him.

People with negative energy, intense suffering, or a bad nature can be relatives, strangers, or enemies. The last thing our self-centered attitude wants to do is to hold them dear as if they were precious treasures. Applying the techniques of thought transformation to our mind, we cease blocking them out as if they didn't have feelings. Instead, we see their humanity. We recognize that they want to be happy and avoid suffering just like we do. We are exactly the same. We open our hearts and recognize that this person is a product of causes and conditions. He's a karmic bubble. He has the potential to become a fully enlightened Buddha.

In *A Guide to the Bodhisattva's Way of Life*, Shantideva says that anger doesn't choose to generate itself. Nor does a person choose to get angry. Someone doesn't think, "I'm going to get angry and send myself to the lower realms." These emotions arise due to causes and conditions. So, instead of hating another person, we practice seeing him as a karmic bubble, that is, as something created by causes and conditions. He hasn't always been who he is now. At one time, he has also been our parent, our lover, our best friend. He's taken care of us and rescued us from danger in previous lives.

Actually, if we look around, people whom we don't like and people who harm us are in the minority. Let's say we're at work, at a social gathering, or at a Dharma center with thirty people. How many of them do we really dislike? We may have problems with a few people here and there, but we manage to stay in a room together, don't we? It's not like we despise them and they hate us. The number of people we can't stand in this world is actually very small. These people are rare. To practice patience we need the people that we don't like. We can't practice patience with our friends or with people who are kind to us. Finding people that we don't like or who threaten us is not so easy. So, when we finally find them, they are a precious treasure! They are rare to find. When we meet them, we can think, "Fantastic, I get to practice patience now."

They say that high-level bodhisattvas pray to meet disgusting, uncooperative people because they want to practice patience. Of course, when you really want to meet obnoxious people, they don't show up! Why don't they turn up for high-level bodhisattvas? Because high-level bodhisattvas don't have any anger. We could be sitting in a room with many people whom we consider unbearable, but high-level bodhisattvas don't see them that way at all. To them, these people appear lovable. Bodhisattvas have such a hard time finding detestable people, whereas we come across them so easily! So, when we find people whom we don't like, feel threatened by, or find despicable, we should recognize that there aren't so many of them around. Therefore, we should cherish them and take the opportunity to practice patience with them.

When we meditate on emptiness, we see there's no inherently existing repulsive person there. What we're seeing is just a karmic bubble appearing due to causes and conditions. That's it. How can we hate a karmic bubble? How can we be disturbed by someone who doesn't really exist in the way she appears to us?

5.   When others, out of jealousy,
     Mistreat me with abuse, slander, and so on,
     I will practice accepting defeat
     And offering the victory to them.

Our first reaction to this verse may be, "This verse is unpatriotic! No upright citizen would ever accept defeat and offer the victory to others!" We've been taught ever since we were children to stick up for ourselves, fight back, and win the fight. People who don't are considered spineless cowards.

Although the verse specifies people who harm us out of jealousy or who abuse or slander us, it may include those who hurt us in other ways, too. Accepting defeat and offering the victory to them doesn't mean that when somebody kicks us, we say, "Sure, go ahead. No problem. Kick me. Beat me to a pulp." We can protect ourselves, but we do so without anger. We protect ourselves using the minimum amount of force possible.

Accepting defeat means we let go of the mind that always wants to have the last word. We realize that we don't have to prove our case. We don't have to make sure that everybody understands that we are right and the other person is wrong. Accepting defeat means letting go of our ego's need to prove itself and be the conqueror.

People can be jealous for a variety of reasons, not just because we have a nicer looking car or a bigger house. They can be jealous because we sit in meditation position longer. Or because we go on more retreats. Or because they think we are closer to the teacher than they are. Or because we have a pink book cover and they have a red one. Our mind can be jealous of anything, you name it! Somebody else has striped socks and we have plain old maroon ones. I'm jealous! Look at what our mind gets jealous about. It's amazing!

So, of course others get jealous, too. If they abuse us to our face, say mean things to us, talk about us behind our back, try to ruin our reputation, gossip, spread rumors about us to other people, instead of going on a crusade to rectify the situation and prove that person is wrong and I am right, we drop the issue. Somebody is gossiping, "blah, blah, blah," and we just drop it because we know that if we start gossiping about them and try to prove our case, we'll add more fuel to the fire. So we remain peaceful inside of ourselves and don't get swept into others' commotion.

There are situations when somebody may spread false stories about us and generate a lot of negativity and misunderstanding in others. In those situations, we need to go to the person and explain what actually happened. We do this not out of attachment to our own reputation, but with care for the person spreading the false stories and concern for the harmony of the group. We don't just sit there and ignore it whenever someone spreads bad stories about us, because sometimes it can harm others to hear them. There are times when we have to explain things, but we do so without blaming the other person.

In summary, if somebody spreads false stories or even true ones about us, and we become angry, upset, or condescending, then mentally we need to "accept defeat," because it is just our ego that dislikes having a bad reputation or being blamed. We need to let go of our attachment to reputation and need for approval, and think, "It's okay if not everyone likes me. I'm okay with it. There's no rule saying that everybody in the world has to like me."

That's different from a situation when somebody makes malicious comments that cause other people to be unnecessarily alarmed, disharmonious, or upset. Such comments incite people to divide into quarreling factions and provoke conflict. In those situations, we need to explain in order to clear the air, but we don't do it by denigrating the other person.

6.   When someone I have benefited
     And in whom I have placed great trust
     Hurts me very badly,
     I will practice seeing that person as my supreme teacher.

The person we have benefited could be our best friend, whom we've trusted and told our secrets to. It could be our child, business partner, neighbor, or sibling. We have been kind to this person and he or she turns around and does something that hurts us. All of us have experienced this, and it can be extremely painful. Of course, we've never done this to anyone else, have we? Because we're really nice people. But we've all had it happen to us. Amazing how we're always kind, generous people and others are always the nasty ones!

When people we've trusted steal our possessions, criticize us, break off a relationship, talk behind our back, stop loving us, or give us bad recommendations, we need to see them as our supreme teacher. What are they teaching us? To abandon expectations. To develop tolerance and the patience that accepts that other people make mistakes. They are sentient beings just like we are, which means they are sometimes overpowered by their confusion, bad judgment, hostility, and clinging attachment, just like we are. They are teaching us to recognize that cyclic existence is not perfect. They are showing us the importance of having compassion and of forgiving.

Sometimes we're hurt because we've given someone more trust than she can bear. For example, we don't trust a toddler with matches because she doesn't yet have the maturity to bear that level of trust. When we give someone more trust than they can bear, it's often due to poor judgment on our part. Swept up with attachment, we exaggerate someone's good qualities and ignore their faults, impairing our judgment and leading us to have false expectations of them. Or, wanting a certain situation to happen very badly, we talk ourselves into trusting someone that we don't know well. Thus when we get hurt, it's a signal that we need to slow down and evaluate people and situations more closely so that we give people the level of trust than they are capable of bearing.

7.   In short, I will offer directly and indirectly
      Every benefit and happiness to all beings, my mothers.
      I will practice in secret taking upon myself
      All their harmful actions and sufferings.

This verse is about *tong–len*, the taking and giving meditation. Geshe Jampa Tegchok gives an excellent explanation of this meditation in his book *Transforming Adversity into Joy and Courage*. We may offer benefit and happiness to others either directly or indirectly. Saying and doing things that affect them positively and lead them on the path directly benefit others; doing the taking and giving meditation indirectly benefits them. This meditation is practiced "in secret" in that we don't arrogantly advertise, "I'm doing a profound meditation in which I take others' suffering upon myself. Aren't I a wonderful, compassionate person for doing this? I'm a bodhisattva in training." Instead of bragging about our meditation practice, we do it privately, without fanfare or conceit.

The taking and giving meditation is part of the system for developing the altruistic intention of bodhicitta called equalizing and exchanging self and others. It is an extremely powerful and beneficial practice which challenges our self-centeredness and enables us to develop strong and stable love and compassion for both ourselves and others. It is a fast way to purify negative karma and create the causes for long life, good health, and both temporary and ultimate happiness.

In the taking and giving practice, we imagine the suffering of others, allowing it to affect us until we find their suffering unbearable and have a strong yearning to be of help. Seeing that what limits us from being able to help is our own self-centeredness, we resolve to mentally take on others' suffering and offer them every happiness they desire in order to subdue our self-preoccupation. Doing this is the opposite of our self-centered view in which we seek benefit and happiness for ourselves and either relegate others' suffering and happiness to second place or ignore them completely. Since our self-centeredness is the enemy that has kept us in suffering states for eons, it is appropriate and desirable to counteract it. Because all our happiness comes due to the kindness of others, it is suitable and beneficial to care about them as much as, if not more than, we care about ourselves.

Because it is so powerful, the taking and giving meditation was considered a secret teaching for many generations. Geshe Chekawa broke the seal of secrecy and taught the practice to, among others, people suffering from leprosy, who were able to cure themselves by doing this practice. Wanting this teaching to be available to others, Geshe Chekawa put it in writing in *The Seven-Point Mind Training*. He practiced this meditation himself and often prayed to be born in the hellish realm for the benefit of others. At his death, he said he had not succeeded in his life work, because a pure realm where no suffering exists appeared to him as he was dying. This pure realm, where he could receive teachings directly from a Buddha and attain full enlightenment, was the result of his sincerely cultivating the heart cherishing others.

Developing bodhicitta is a challenging process. To produce the mind that desires that all beings, without exception, be free of suffering and have true happiness, even at our own expense, is not easy. What makes it difficult? Self-grasping ignorance, the mental factor that holds all persons and phenomena to exist from their own side, with their own inherent nature, independent of causes and conditions, parts, and the mind that conceives and labels them. Because we cling to our innate, deeply embedded belief in a truly existent "me," we seek our own happiness at all costs. From this arise attachment, hostility, jealousy, arrogance, and other disturbing attitudes and negative emotions. The more we seek to protect and defend this independent self and search for our own happiness, the more unhappy we are. This is clear when we examine our own experiences. However, self-grasping ignorance and its cohort, self-centeredness, are misplaced because no solid, truly existent, findable self exists.

When doing the taking and giving practice, we begin by taking suffering, and before taking on the suffering of others we begin with taking on our own future misery. In the space in front, imagine yourself in the future, as an old person, ill, feeble, alone, and afraid of death. Generate strong compassion for your future self, wishing him or her to be free from this suffering. Imagine all that suffering emerging from your future self in the form of a dense smoke or pollution and feel the relief your future self feels from the alleviation of that misery. Imagine inhaling that smoke and it transforming into lightning or a thunderbolt which then crashes into your own disturbing attitudes and negative emotions visualized as a hard lump at your heart. That lump of ignorance and self-centeredness is obliterated due to the force of your compassion for your future self.

Feel the softness and openness at your heart—the absence of the painful lump of self-centeredness. Stay in that open space, free of your ordinary self-grasping and self-preoccupation for as long as you can.

Within that open space at your heart a beautiful light appears. That light is your love and it radiates and gently falls onto your future self as you give your future self whatever it needs to be happy. Rest for a moment with this sense of relief and release and kindness toward yourself.

Then think of someone for whom you feel natural, spontaneous affection. As the image of that person comes to mind, picture something that you know gives him mental or physical pain or discomfort. Imagine how he feels and generate a genuine sense of compassion for him. Resolve to take this suffering on yourself so that he will be free from it.

Using the image of smoke or pollution, breathe the suffering of the person you love into your heart. Take not only his suffering, but also the causes of suffering—his disturbing attitudes, negative emotions, and negative karmic imprints. If he suffers due to his own anger, imagine taking his rage. Take his attachment, bitterness, grudges, loneliness, anxiety, and guilt visualized as smoke or pollution. That transforms into a thunderbolt which destroys the rotten lump of self-centeredness at your own heart. Through this skillful method you take their suffering and its causes, which is what they don't want, and use them to crush your own self-grasping and self-centeredness, which is the cause of your own suffering.

Stay in that relaxed spaciousness for a while. Then the brilliant light of your love appears at your heart. Send that out to your dear one. Imagine transforming your body, possessions, and positive potential into whatever he needs and give it to him. He receives everything he needs and experiences happiness and satisfaction. You in turn experience joy at their happiness.

Then turn your mind to a stranger: a homeless person you saw recently and felt confused about how best to help them, a person you saw driving who had a look of sadness about her. You could think of a group —people in a war-torn country, all those suffering from cancer, victims of floods or fire. It could be people with a particularly difficult health problem, or animals. Do the same meditation described above to take their suffering and give them your happiness.

Continue by doing taking and giving for people you don't like and finally for all sentient beings everywhere. It's important each time to use their misery to destroy the cause of your own misery, self-grasping ignorance and self-centeredness. Similarly, each time imagine transforming your body, possessions, and positive potential into every temporal and ultimate happiness they could want and give it to them. Give food to the hungry, water to the thirsty, good health to the sick, rest to the weary and overworked, wealth to the poor, sun and rain to the farmers, safe places to sleep to the homeless, freedom from addiction to the chemically dependent, relief from emotional pain to those who are fearful, anxious, depressed, or grieving; comfort and care to the dying, and Dharma teachings and conducive circumstances for practicing them to each being.

Whatever is needed to ease the distress of beings flows out from your heart and is received by those in need. Include in that offering all your own good fortune, causes of happiness, efforts in practice, virtues and talents, and all your aspirations to reach greater clarity of mind and, ultimately, Buddhahood. Imagine all beings receiving what they need, progressing on the path, and becoming Buddhas.

Rejoice in the happiness that you have given them and feel joy from having relinquished your own self-centeredness. Rejoice at awakening this new state of mind, and determine to cultivate this altruistic wish to help all beings in every way you possibly can.

This practice is especially good to do when we are unhappy or ill. Instead of feeling sorry for ourselves, which only exacerbates our misery, we turn our focus to those who have similar problems. Generating compassion for them, we think, "As long as I am sick (or unhappy), may what I am experiencing suffice for the sickness and unhappiness of all others." Then take on their illness and depression and meditate as above. Feel that by your experiencing the misery that is present in your life at the moment all others are freed from theirs. Feel their relief; be joyful that you are able to do this for them. When you imagine giving them your body, possessions, and positive potential, which have all been transformed into what they need for temporal and ultimate happiness, experience their happiness. Be joyful that you are able to contribute to their well-being and rejoice at the physical and mental peace they experience. Dedicate the positive potential accumulated from doing this practice for the enlightenment of all sentient beings.

People sometimes worry that if they visualize taking on others' sufferings, they will suffer more. They fear they will get sick or inherit others' negative karma. A great deal of resistance may come up when we think of taking others' suffering onto ourselves and giving away our body, possessions, and positive potential so they will be happy. Dealing with this resistance is a crucial part of the taking and giving practice. It is important to ease into the practice rather than set up walls against it. When resistance arises, contemplate the following:

1. Each of us experiences the results of our own actions, or karma, not the results of others' karma. Therefore, we will not increase our suffering by imagining taking on others'.

2. It is simply our self-centeredness that is creating the fuss. This self-centeredness has consistently been our enemy and the source of all our suffering and problems. When our enemy is harmed we rejoice. Likewise, when our self-centeredness feels uncomfortable, we can say, "Good!" because we know we are opposing the source of our suffering.

3. We have received amazing kindness and benefit from others. Everything we have and all our talents come due to their care and efforts. Seeing this clearly, the wish to repay their kindness will naturally arise.

4. Genuinely cherishing others —which is to be differentiated from pleasing people because we seek their love and approval—brings only benefit, whereas self-centeredness causes suffering.

The taking and giving practice brings a sense of tremendous spaciousness and joy, and a great sense of relief knowing that we can mentally do something powerful to help others and at the same time loosen the hold of our self-centered attitude.

8.   Without these practices being defiled by the stains of the eight
       worldly concerns,
    By perceiving all phenomena as illusory,
    I will practice without grasping to release all beings
    From the bondage of the disturbing unsubdued mind and
       karma.

This verse concerns meditating on emptiness. It's easy to practice the Dharma with one or more of the eight worldly concerns lurking in our mind. These eight, which seek the happiness of only this life, are attachment to material possessions and money, praise and approval, good reputation, and pleasures of the six senses, and aversion to losing material possessions and money, receiving blame or disapproval, having a bad reputation, and having unpleasant experiences. "*Without these practices being defiled by the stains of the eight worldly concerns*" means not doing the above practices with the hope of receiving money, possessions, approval, praise, fame, or pleasant sensory experiences or the wish to avoid difficulties in this life.

We dispel the eight worldly concerns by perceiving all phenomena as illusory. That is, they do not exist in the way they appear to. To perceive all phenomena as illusory, first we meditate on their emptiness. After arising from that meditation, we recognize the appearance of inherent existence as false. While persons and phenomena appear to exist inherently, with their own immutable essence, they do not. Their appearance is deceptive; it is like an illusion. By seeing things as illusionlike, we practice without any grasping at an inherently existent "I" or "mine." Similarly, our grasping at inherently existent phenomena ceases as well. Through this, we release ourselves from the bondage of the disturbing unsubdued mind and karma and thereby become more skillful in releasing others from this bondage. We lead others to liberation by teaching them the Dharma, guiding them on the path, inspiring them through our example, encouraging them, and being a friend. To do that, we have to practice sincerely and continuously in order to integrate the teachings with our mind.

5 Purifying and Receiving Inspiration

FRONT GENERATION AND SELF-GENERATION

IN FRONT GENERATION PRACTICE, we remain in our ordinary form and visualize the deity in front of us, above our head or in our heart chakra. In self-generation, we dissolve in emptiness, and our wisdom realizing emptiness appears in the form of the deity with whom we then identify.

To do the self-generation of Thousand-Arm Chenrezig, you must have received the *wong* or initiation (empowerment) into Thousand-Arm Chenrezig. This is usually a two-day ceremony, in which one enters the mandala of Thousand-Arm Chenrezig. A *wong* is different from a *jenang*, which is a permission or a blessing of the deity's body, speech, and mind. A *jenang* is a short, one-day ceremony. The *jenang* of four-arm Chenrezig and the *jenang* of two-arm Chenrezig are not the same as a *wong* of Thousand-Arm Chenrezig. Only those who have received the *wong* of Thousand-Arm Chenrezig may do the self-generation practice, which begins with the "Ultimate Nature of the Deity." Everyone else should continue with the sadhana, meditating on the section "Those who have not received the great empowerment into the Chenrezig mandala," which contains purification and receiving inspiration as well as absorbing Chenrezig into you.

The next section of purification may be practiced by everyone, both those doing the front generation and those doing the self-generation. However, it is fine if those doing the self-generation wish to skip this purification section and go directly to the self-generation practice so that they will have more time to meditate on it.

PURIFICATION AND RECEIVING INSPIRATION

The visualization for purification and receiving inspiration is pretty straightforward—it is as described in the sadhana. Chenrezig comes from the space in front of you to the top of your head, facing the same direction as you do. It's as if Chenrezig is now an extension of yourself, resting on top of your head and looking over you with kindness. Imagine that Chenrezig also appears on the head of each sentient being, who are all seated around you. At the heart of each Chenrezig is a small, horizontal lotus, upon which rests a flat moon disk. Standing upright at the center of the moon is the seed syllable HRIH, the essence of Chenrezig's omniscient mind of wisdom and compassion. In other words, all of Chenrezig's magnificent realizations appear in the form of the radiant syllable HRIH. The HRIH is surrounded by the syllables of the long mantra, which stand upright near the edge of the moon disk. Between them and the HRIH stand the syllables of the six-syllable mantra, OM MANI PADME HUM. All the Chenrezigs, lotuses, moons, mantra syllables, and HRIHs are made of radiant light.

From the mantra syllables and HRIH much white light and nectar, representing the nature of Chenrezig's blissful omniscient mind, flow into you, permeating every cell of your body. There's nowhere in your body or mind that is untouched by this compassionate light and nectar. Your entire nervous system experiences bliss. This bliss is not the agitated kind that makes us crave more, but is a gentle bliss in which we feel 100% satisfied and content. The light and nectar totally purify all disturbing attitudes and emotions, negative karmic imprints, diseases, and obscurations. Feel completely pure and blissful. The light and nectar also fill you with all the realizations of the gradual path to enlightenment, especially Chenrezig's love, compassion, and wisdom.

Similarly, light and nectar from the Chenrezigs on the crowns of all the sentient beings flow into them, purifying all negativities and obscurations and inspiring them with all the realizations of the path to enlightenment.

Recite the mantras as many times as you wish to while continuing to do this visualization. If it's easier for you, spend some time just focusing on the visualization without saying the mantra. Then add the mantra when you're ready to. You can say the mantra silently to yourself or whisper it out loud. If you're alone or if you're doing the practice with a group of other people, all of you may want to recite the mantras out loud in unison. The sound of the mantra being recited in this way is very powerful and helps you to focus on the meditation.

An important factor in the visualization is to allow the light and nectar into you. Don't strain and try to see it with your eyes. Don't try too hard to feel blissful. Just relax and let Chenrezig's compassion and blissful energy fill you up.

I used to feel that I couldn't do this kind of meditation very well. It seemed to me that when my teacher led a sadhana and said, "Feel blissful," everyone else in the room looked idyllic while I felt nothing, except maybe pain in my knees. I would try to force myself to feel blissful and then feel like a failure because I didn't. This is not the right approach! But when I relaxed and "played" with the visualization instead of taking it and myself so seriously, some feeling for Chenrezig began to come.

Let the blissful light and nectar purify your body and mind. Sometimes we think that we don't deserve to feel joyful. Ego says, "You've created so much negative karma, you should feel guilty and remorseful and hang your head in shame. How can you feel blissful when you're such a sinner?" This is our old Judeo-Christian baggage in which we mistakenly think, "Unless I'm miserable, I can't purify. Unless I suffer, I'm not truly cherishing others. If I feel good, it's selfish." This is old conditioning that doesn't make much sense. It's important that we let such misconceptions surface so that we can identify them and then evaluate if their content is true or not. If it isn't, then let go of that belief.

For example, we may have the unrecognized preconception, "If I feel guilty and hate myself, I'm atoning for the harms I've caused others." Is this true? How can feeling guilty erase negative karma? Guilt and self-hatred are disturbing emotions that keep us locked in patterns of useless behavior. Rather than purify negative karma, they create more of it.

There's nothing wrong with feeling happy. Isn't happiness and peace what we all desire? We shouldn't feel guilty and undeserving for being blissful when Chenrezig's light and nectar flow into us. Instead, the bliss lightens the burden of negative karma, which in turn enables us to feel more content. With a satisfied, peaceful mind, our attitude towards life transforms as do our actions. Feeling lighter inside ourselves, we will treat others more respectfully and be less demanding and more gener- ous to them.

ABSORPTION

After reciting the mantras, make the strong determination, *"I will live my life in a meaningful way, and do all actions with the motivation to attain enlightenment for the benefit of all sentient beings."* Then Chen- rezig absorbs into you. Concentrate on your body being clean and clear like unstained crystal and your mind being united with Chenrezig's qualities such as love, compassion, patience, and wisdom.

This practice is quite a profound psychological method. First we project Chenrezig in front of us. Then we take refuge, generate bodhi- citta, create positive potential and purify our negative actions, set our highest aspirations by making requests, meditate on *The Eight Verses*, and purify and receive Chenrezig's inspiration. Now Chenrezig absorbs into us, illustrating that Chenrezig comes from our mind: Chenrezig exists in dependence upon and in relationship to the mind.

You may do the sadhana as a guru yoga practice. This means medi- tating that Chenrezig is not only the embodiment of all the Buddhas, Dharma, and Sangha, but also the nature of the ultimate guru. The ultimate guru is the transcendental wisdom of bliss and emptiness, which appears in diverse forms according to the dispositions of various sentient beings. This transcendental wisdom can appear as Chenrezig and as our spiritual mentor. The nature of our spiritual mentor (transcendental wisdom) appears as Chenrezig, and the nature of Chenrezig appears as our spiritual mentor. When we think of our teacher as being the same nature as Chenrezig, we will pay closer attention to the teachings he or she gives and will follow his or her guidance more closely. This helps us to take the teachings more seriously and to practice them more diligently.

Seeing our spiritual mentor as Chenrezig does not mean we project all sorts of fantasies onto him or her. "My teacher is Buddha so I don't need to tell him anything because he has clairvoyance and knows everything." "My teacher is Buddha so I don't need to take her to the doctor when she's sick." It also doesn't mean we worship the personality of the teacher. Sometimes I think that in the name of being committed to our teachers, we project even more inherent existence onto them, building them up to be the object of our fantasies. This only leads to confusion and disappointment.

When Chenrezig dissolves into us, we feel that Chenrezig, the Three Jewels, the transcendental wisdom of bliss and emptiness, and the transcendental aspect of our spiritual mentor all dissolve into us. We feel very close to our teacher, close to the wisdom of bliss and emptiness, close to the Buddhas, Dharma, and Sangha. We feel that our minds have become like Chenrezig's, with the same realizations, the same peace, calm, and openness. We feel that our body has become clear and pure. Instead of being heavy, hungry, and dissatisfied, our body feels light, comfortable, and flexible.

At the conclusion of your meditation, dedicate the positive potential of your practice by reciting and contemplating the dedication verses at the end of the sadhana.

6 *Meditating on Emptiness*

ALL THE PRACTICES until now have been pre-liminaries to the self-generation, which is the heart of the practice. These preliminaries are incredibly important; we shouldn't neglect them. Spend as much time as you want on them. They make the self-generation more alive and vibrant.

Self-generation as Chenrezig may be done by those who have received the empowerment of Thousand-Arm Chenrezig. The process of self-generation is done in six steps, called the six deities: the Ultimate Nature of the Deity, and the Deities of Sound, Letter, Form, Mudra, and Sign. Calling these six "deities" doesn't mean that they are different Buddha figures that we visualize. Rather, they are guiding us to see the essence of the deity—the transcendental wisdom of bliss and emptiness—in six different ways. This helps us to avoid considering Chenrezig as an inherently existent deity or person out there that we worship.

THE FIRST DEITY:
THE ULTIMATE NATURE OF THE DEITY

The first deity is the Ultimate Nature of the Deity. Here we meditate on the emptiness of ourselves and the emptiness of the deity.

Sadhanas don't spell out everything in words. For example, the line OM SVABHAVA SHUDDHA SARVA DHARMA SVABHAVA SHUDDHO HAM is not very many words. If you like to chant, you might chant that mantra and keep going, overlooking the emptiness meditation that is to be done at that point. For that reason, we need to receive teachings on the sadhana so that we will know how to meditate and at what points to stop and meditate in depth.

The mantra OM SVABHAVA SHUDDHA SARVA DHARMA SVABHAVA SHUDDHO HAM means, "By essential nature, all phenomena are pure. By essential nature, I am pure." This mantra has great significance; it speaks about "essential nature," which is the deeper way in which things exist. This is ultimate truth, the emptiness of inherent existence of all phenomena. By nature all phenomena lack inherent existence, which means that they're pure of existing from their own side. They lack any inherent nature or findable essence and don't exist independently; they don't exist under their own power, but depend on other factors to exist.

"The nature of myself, of the meditational deity, and of all phenomena is pure in the one taste of emptiness." Just as one spoonful of sugar has the same taste as another spoonful of sugar—their tastes can't be differentiated, similarly, the emptiness of the "I," the emptiness of Chenrezig, and the emptiness of all phenomena can't be differentiated experientially. They are one taste. To a wisdom that cognizes emptiness nonconceptually, there's no difference between the emptiness of Chenrezig, the emptiness of all phenomena, and the emptiness of the self. When the mind is in meditative equipoise on emptiness, there's no discrimination between the emptiness of one thing and the emptiness of another. We and Chenrezig are equal in being empty. During meditative equipoise on emptiness, there's no appearance of conventional phenomena, such as "me," Chenrezig, or anything else. During this meditative equipoise, the mind is completely absorbed in the nondual experience of the lack of inherent existence.

"Nondual" has several meanings. One is emptiness of inherent existence; another is the absence of an appearance of subject and object as different entities. In the direct realization of emptiness, there is no thought, "I'm meditating on emptiness." There is no feeling of a separate observer, "I," who is realizing, and object, emptiness. Experientially, the mind is fused with the emptiness of inherent existence, the ultimate nature of all things that exist.

Note that we don't say the subject and object are one. "One" is an ambiguous word. It is not the same as "nondual" because "one" indicates a collection of things. As soon as we say "one," multiplicity is implied, because "one" is discerned in relationship to multiplicity, or more than one. In contrast, the word "nondual" implies lack of duality and nothing more. In other words, nothing else is asserted when inherent existence is negated. For this reason, the emptiness of inherent existence is said to be a nonaffirming negation, as nothing else is implied or affirmed when inherent existence is negated.

Saying or feeling, "I am one with everything" doesn't imply emptiness. There's still an "I," except now it increases in size and spreads throughout the whole universe because it's one with everything. The "I" hasn't disappeared, it's enlarged. It's more accurate to think, "The ultimate nature of Chenrezig and my ultimate nature are nondual. My wisdom and Chenrezig's wisdom realizing emptiness become inseparable. There is no inherently existent 'I' or inherently existent 'other.'" This reminds us that emptiness is not an affirmative phenomenon, as "they become one" implies. It is a nonaffirming negation.

The meditation on the ultimate nature of the deity helps us to prepare for death. At the time we die, our gross five aggregates gradually lose power, and the mind becomes subtler. When we ordinary beings realize that we're dying, we cling strongly to this life, particularly to this body. We freak out: "If I leave this body, this ego-identity, who will I be?" There's tremendous craving to remain connected to this body, to this ego-identity, and to this world. In the twelve links of dependent arising, this is the eighth link, craving. Then, at a certain point in the death process, we realize we are going to have to separate from our body and ego-identity. So what does our ignorance do? It grasps at another body and ego-identity. That's the ninth link, grasping. The craving and grasping nourish previously created karma so that it ripens. This is the tenth link, becoming.

During our life, many karmic seeds have been planted on our mindstream because we've done so many actions throughout our life. The first of the twelve links—the ignorance that misconceives the nature of reality—begins this process. It gives rises to various disturbing attitudes and negative emotions. These motivate the second link, actions. These actions, or karma, leave seeds on the mindstream; this is the third link. The craving and grasping that arise during the death process fertilize some seeds so that they begin to sprout. This is the tenth link, becoming, which propels the next rebirth. Once more we get contaminated aggregates—the fourth link called "name and form"—and are born in cyclic existence—the eleventh link, birth. Six sense sources, contact, and feeling—the fifth, sixth, and seventh links—follow soon thereafter. As soon as we are born, aging, sickness, and death come along. They are the twelfth link. In addition, since ignorance still exists in our mindstream, it gives rise to more karma, which leaves more karmic seeds, which produce more births. This is the cycle called samsara, or cyclic existence.

I encourage you to study the twelve links of dependent arising in more depth. What is explained above is very general. You may be wondering why I didn't explain the twelve links in numerical order; a more extensive explanation will clarify that doubt. The teaching on the twelve links may sound very technical the first time we hear it, but when we contemplate it in terms of our own experience, it really wakes us up to the seriousness of our situation in cyclic existence.

The time of death is an opportunity to stop the cycle of the twelve links. If we're able to stop craving and grasping at that time, there's a possibility to stop the ripening of karmic seeds and subsequent rebirth. If we meditate on emptiness while we are dying, we won't generate fear as we separate from this body and ego-identity, because we'll recognize that all these do not exist inherently. We'll know that there's no real "I" to protect, and there's no inherently existent body to cling to. In fact, there's no truly existent person who's dying. There's no truly existent external pleasure or suffering to grasp at or repel. The meditation on emptiness makes dying easy.

When very advanced practitioners die, it's like going on a picnic. They have such a good time. It's so relaxing. They don't worry about losing their body or ego-identity. They don't worry about what their future rebirth will be because their mind understands reality. So, when they die, it's so blissful; they have a great time.

I saw one old monk in Dharamsala die like that. He wasn't a geshe or a rinpoche, just an ordinary monk, but the way he died made a strong impression on me. He was so relaxed and knew exactly what to do. Accomplished practitioners do strong meditation while dying and at the time of death. For example, my ordination master, Ling Rinpoche, stayed in meditation for thirteen days after his breath stopped. His body was sitting upright, but there was no breath although there was a little warmth at his heart chakra. He meditated in clear light for thirteen days. His death was incredibly blissful with no fear or anxiety. Training well in this first step, the Ultimate Nature of the Deity, will enable us to soothe difficulties during life, banish the fear of death, and attain enlightenment.

Buddha-nature

Meditating to develop the wisdom realizing emptiness is important because it is this wisdom that can decisively remove all defilements from our mindstream, enabling us to attain liberation and enlightenment. Why can defilments be eliminated from the mind? Because they are based on ignorance and once ignorance is eliminated by the wisdom realizing emptiness, the defilements lose their foundation. How can our mind be transformed into the mind of a Buddha? Because we have the Buddha-nature.

There are two types of Buddha-nature: the natural Buddha-nature and the evolutionary Buddha-nature. The natural Buddha-nature—the emptiness of inherent existence of our mind—becomes the nature dharmakaya, or nature truth body, of a Buddha. The evolutionary Buddha-nature becomes the wisdom dharmakaya, or wisdom truth body, of a Buddha. The nature truth body is the true cessations and emptiness of inherent existence of a Buddha's mind. The wisdom truth body is a Buddha's omniscient mind—a mind that is completely cleansed of defilements and imbued with all good qualities that have been developed limitlessly.

Sometimes people have the idea that Buddha-nature is something like a soul. When they say, "I have Buddha-nature," they feel as if there's a real self or soul that's pure inside of them. It's almost like saying, "We have God inside of us," and thinking there's an essence inside each person that is inherently divine. We're still thinking that something about ourselves is inherently real and findable. But the natural Buddha-nature is emptiness. It is a negation; it's the absence of inherent existence, which is a nonaffirming negation. Nothing at all is being affirmed: emptiness is the mere absence of inherent existence.

The natural Buddha-nature is the emptiness of inherent existence of our mind. All phenomena by their very nature are pure of inherent existence. We, also, are pure of inherent existence. Because our mind is empty of inherent existence, we have the potential to become Buddhas. If we or our mind were to exist independently, with its own immutable nature, then we could not change. If we were inherently existent, there would be no possibility to change, and becoming a Buddha would be impossible.

In fact, if inherent existence were the ultimate nature of phenomena, it would be impossible for anything to exist at all. If things had an inherent essence, if they had their own nature from their own side, independent of everything else, then nothing could affect them; nothing could make them change. We see, however, that we and the things around us change all the time. Just the fact that we change indicates that we don't exist independently. It means that we depend on causes and conditions. When causes and conditions change, we change. Thus, this feeling we have of being a real person with an inherent essence is totally false. We don't exist in that way at all. This lack of inherent existence of our mind is our natural Buddha-nature.

The other kind of Buddha-nature is called the evolutionary Buddha-nature. This includes all the factors in our mind that can transform into the qualities of the Buddha's wisdom dharmakaya. There's a section on Buddha-nature in *Open Heart, Clear Mind* that explains this in more depth. Included in this evolutionary Buddha-nature is the clear light conventional nature of the mind, i.e., the clear and aware conventional nature of the mind that can reflect and engage in objects. The evolutionary Buddha-nature also includes mental factors such as love, compassion, wisdom, concentration, and so forth—beneficial mental factors that can be developed infinitely. The continuity of these mental factors and of the luminous and aware nature of mind become the wisdom dharmakaya of a Buddha.

Our empty nature becomes the nature dharmakaya of the Buddha, the emptiness and cessation of suffering and its origins of a Buddha's mind. Understanding this is important because it enables us to understand how it's possible to go from where we are now to enlightenment. It's not make-believe, nor do we go "Poof!" and become a Buddha. You can actually see how the fundamental factors necessary for enlightenment exist now and how they just need to be revealed and developed. There's a progression, a continuity, and a transformation so that our two Buddha-natures become the different Buddha-bodies. When we understand this, we develop faith and confidence that enlightenment is actually possible.

Emptiness

The emptiness of inherent existence is called the purity of phenomena, including the purity of ourselves. All appearances that we experience now—the appearance of cyclic existence, our lives filled with problems and suffering—do not exist in the way they appear to us. We and everything around us appear to be so real, and we assent to this appearance, grasping at everything as existing from its own side. However, when we investigate more deeply and look beyond appearances, we realize that it's impossible for things to exist in the way they appear. Seeing this gives us a kind of spaciousness and freedom because, if samsara were inherently existent and everything really did exist the way it appears to us, then transformation and change could not occur. If a jerk were inherently a jerk, and a promotion were inherently desirable, and chocolate were inherently delicious, then nothing could ever change, and the best we could ever have is what we have right now. Thinking about the emptiness of inherent existence shows us the possibility for change. Beauty can come forth because nothing is inherently concrete, fixed, or findable.

Our mind needs to stretch to encompass emptiness. Our minds are so stuck in the idea, "Things exist the way they appear to me. What I see is reality. It is 100 percent true. There's nothing to doubt. Things exist exactly as they appear to my senses, exactly as they appear to my mental consciousness." We hardly ever doubt that. Not only do we have the appearance of inherent existence to our sense consciousnesses and mental consciousness, but also our mental consciousness grasps on to that appearance and says, "Yes! Everything really exists in this findable, independent way. Everything is real as it appears to me."

When we believe there's a real "me," then we have to protect that self and bring it happiness. Thus, we are attached to things that are pleasurable and become angry at anything unpleasant. Pride, jealousy, laziness, and the whole gamut of negative emotions follow. Motivated by these, we act physically, verbally, and mentally. These actions, or karma, leave seeds on our mindstream, and when these ripen, they influence what we experience. We again relate to these experiences ignorantly, so more emotions arise, motivating us to create more karma. As a result, cyclic existence with all its difficulties continues on and on, created by our mind, dependent on the ignorance that misconceives the nature of ourselves and all other phenomena.

In the Ultimate Nature of the Deity, we meditate on the emptiness of ourselves and the emptiness of Chenrezig, the emptiness of samsara and the emptiness of nirvana, the emptiness of all phenomena. Sometimes, we think, "Okay, I'm empty of inherent existence—but Chenrezig is inherently existent!" We make Chenrezig into something like God. Instead of God in Heaven, we think, "There's Chenrezig in a Sukhavati Pure Land." Although the words we use are different, our conception may be similar: we believe there is an inherently existent, powerful divine being out there who will save us.

While some people may relate to Chenrezig as if he were an inherently existent external person, that is not who Chenrezig is. Chenrezig also has no inherent nature and exists by depending on other factors. What does Chenrezig depend on? Chenrezig is designated in dependence on a body and mind. His is not a flesh-and-blood body like ours and not a mind contaminated by afflictions like ours. Rather, in dependence upon a pure body and mind, the name "Chenrezig" is merely imputed, and thus Chenrezig exists. Even enlightenment isn't inherently existent. It's a state that is labeled in dependence on certain qualities. When these qualities exist, we label "enlightenment" in dependence on them. When a pure mind and a body of light that appears with eleven heads and a thousand arms exist, we label "Chenrezig."

So, Chenrezig isn't inherently existent. Even the emptiness of ourselves and the emptiness of Chenrezig aren't inherently existent. Sometimes our mind gets tangled up and thinks, "I'm empty and Chenrezig is empty; but emptiness exists inherently. It is an absolute truth that exists independent of everything else."

Emptiness also exists by being merely labeled and by depending on the objects that are empty. It depends on the mind that conceives and labels it. For the emptiness of a phenomenon to exist, that phenomenon must exist. Emptiness is not empty space like an empty refrigerator or an empty bank account. Emptiness is the lack of inherent existence. A conventionally existing phenomenon must exist for its emptiness to exist. We couldn't meditate on the emptiness of Susan if Susan were totally nonexistent. If something, like a rabbit's horn, didn't exist at all, we couldn't talk about its emptiness. Thus emptiness, too, is dependent, in this case on the conventionally existent phenomenon which it is the emptiness of. On the basis of the reasoning consciousness analyzing the ultimate not finding an inherently existent car, "the emptiness of the car" is labeled.

Emptiness is also not nothingness. It doesn't mean nothing exists, for that would be the extreme view of nihilism. Nor does meditating on emptiness mean making our mind blank and perceiving nothing. Such meditation just makes our mind dull and spaced-out. This state is far from realizing the ultimate nature of phenomena.

Realizing something is empty doesn't mean we destroy something about that object and create emptiness in its place. Rather, emptiness is the lack of something that never existed to start with. When we meditate on emptiness, we don't destroy inherent existence, because inherent existence has never existed. We're destroying the concept that grasps at inherent existence, what we call self-grasping ignorance. That grasping exists in us ordinary beings, but what it grasps at—inherently existent phenomena—don't exist at all. Meanwhile, what actually exists, emptiness, is more subtle and is difficult for us to ascertain. Furthermore, realizing conventional truths as conventional truths is even more difficult. We don't comprehend what it means to exist by merely being labeled, to exist dependently, to exist conventionally. No wonder we have so many problems! We don't understand either conventional truths or ultimate truths correctly.

When we contemplate this, it becomes clear how much our mind hallucinates, what it means to be in samsara, and how completely off-base our mind is. We can be so convinced that something really exists when it does not exist at all. It's hard for us even to doubt our wrong views and the mistaken appearances that appear to our minds. Instead, we think that everything we perceive exists as it appears, and we believe that everything we think and feel is accurate.

For example, when we watch a movie on television, we relate to the characters as if they were real people. Attachment surfaces when the hero and heroine kiss; fear or hostility arises when there is violence in the film. Producers make sure there is an emotional high point every few minutes, otherwise the film is considered boring, and we comply by generating all sorts of emotional reactions in response to what the characters do and experience. But are there real people in that box on the table in front of us? Of course not. There's just the appearance of people; in fact there is only a screen with designs on it. Of course we know this intellectually, but look how many feelings whirl in our mind when we relate to the appearance of real people as true.

The Heart of the Practice

This Ultimate Nature of the Deity, the first of the six yogas, is the heart of the Chenrezig Yoga Method. If we don't meditate on emptiness, we might visualize ourselves as Chenrezig, say ten zillion mantras, and do a fire puja at the end of a retreat, but we haven't really meditated on the Chenrezig Yoga Method. Deity yoga practice is founded on emptiness; it exists within emptiness. In the practice, we visualize things manifesting, light radiating, and Chenrezig and goddesses appearing and reabsorbing. It seems like there's a whole lot going on. But, in actual fact, the entire practice is a meditation on the inseparability of emptiness and dependent arising. We meditate on emptiness at the very beginning so that we remember that everything else we visualize later arises within emptiness. Everything we visualize is empty of inherent existence. Furthermore, we contemplate that our wisdom realizing emptiness appears as the deity, all the offering objects, offering goddesses, etc.

Thus, meditating on emptiness before generating ourselves as Chenrezig is important. If we don't do this part well, or if we just skim over it, we miss so much. In some of the Tibetan monasteries, the monks say, "OM PADMANTA KRI TA HUM PHAT. OM SVABHAVA SHUDDHA SARVA DHARMA SVABHAVA SHUDDHO HAM. Everything is empty. Within emptiness..." and without missing a beat, they go on to the visualization. Nobody stops to meditate on emptiness. When they teach, the lamas say, "Hey, everyone! You need to stop here and meditate." But somehow when they do the practice together in a group, they don't. I think it's better that we follow the instructions of the lamas and pause here to meditate on emptiness.

Meditating on emptiness involves examining some of our deepest beliefs. We don't even recognize our beliefs to be beliefs because we assume that's the way things are. Some of our deepest beliefs are our beliefs about ourselves. We have innate beliefs or preconceptions, one of which is the self-grasping we're born with. Even babies have this feeling or concept of a solid "me." Although they don't say it in words, their minds grasp themselves as inherently existent. Their world centers on themselves. Babies want this and don't want that. This innate concept of a findable, inherently existent "I" existed before we were even born in this life.

As we grow up, we pile on all sorts of additional self-concepts. We're full of self-concepts, and we believe every one of them is true! Therapy deals with some of the grosser level of self-concepts, but doesn't touch the innate level. The grosser level includes identities and beliefs about ourselves that are based on our race, ethnicity, and gender. For example, whether we're female or male, it's hard to imagine ourselves being the other gender. We have strong concepts: "I am a woman. Therefore a, b, c," or "I am a man. Therefore x, y, z," and we relate to the whole world through that filter.

Sometimes when doing deity yoga, we have a hard time imagining ourselves as a male deity if we're women, or as a female deity if we're men. It feels funny. We don't feel like "me" anymore. That shows us how much we grasp at our gender as part of our self-identity. Whereas grasping at the inherent existence of our gender is innate ignorance, developing a self-concept of what it means to be a certain gender is acquired—we learn it in this life. We also grasp at our nationality, race, sexual orientation, social class, educational background, and economic status, and we create identities around them. In addition, we have other self-images such as, "I'm stupid," "I'm talented," "I can never do this," "I am always like that."

One reason we get into difficulties with other people is that they don't always agree with our concept of ourselves. We're so sure that our self-concepts are who we are that we get upset when others don't agree: "Don't tell me who I am! I live with me. I know who I am. Your idea about me is all wrong!" If we think we're great and somebody criticizes us, they're wrong. If we think we're totally unlovable and someone loves us, we won't let them: "I'm not lovable. What kind of idiot would love me?"

We hold on to these subconscious self-concepts as if they were totally true. We never doubt them. By meditating on the Ultimate Nature of the Deity, we call these self-concepts into question. We examine each and every one of them. We might say, "Well, okay, I'm not my race, I'm not my profession, I'm not my gender, but I really am unlovable. That's my ultimate nature." Or, "I really am intelligent," or "I really am a Dharma nerd." Whatever it is, we believe, "*This* is who I am."

We might even peel away all those identities but still think, "I'm not a Dharma nerd, but there is a real essence that is 'me.' There's a raw feeling of 'me-ness.'" We have to get in touch with that and examine if the "I" actually exists in this way. That is, an inherently existent "I" appears to us, but instead of assenting to that appearance and holding it to be true, we analyze how the "I" actually exists.

At those times in our life when there's a very solid feeling of "I," it's helpful to examine how that "I" appears. I remember the first time I stayed out all night in college and my mother didn't know. I came home the next day with this feeling that "I" really existed: "I did this and my mother doesn't know!" The feeling of "I" was just enormous, incredibly solid, because I did something I wasn't supposed to do.

Examine how that "I" appears, that big "I," especially when you have a strong emotion. Get familiar with that sense of "I." When somebody criticizes us or accuses us of doing something that we didn't do, this feeling comes up very quickly. Usually, we're focused not on the feeling of "I," but on attacking the other person or escaping from him. But if we can step back, it's an incredible opportunity to study the feeling of "I." The person who irritates us the most can be our best Dharma asset because he gives us an opportunity to look at this sense of "I."

When somebody gives us advice that we don't want to listen to, observe the feeling of "I" that arises. It feels as if there's a real "me" in there, doesn't it? There's a real "I," and that "I" knows how to run my life and doesn't want any advice. That "I" says, "Give me what I want but don't tell me what to do." The "I" appears very strongly when we're under the sway of anger or jealousy. We're sure it exists in the way it appears to.

When we're very attached to something, the sense of a solid "I" pops up. For example, you finally meet Buddha-boy. Finally, he has come to the Dharma center. "Wow! Buddha-boy is here! Not only is he here, but he likes me." Me! Me! And the "I" gets incredibly big. Investigate how that "I" appears at this time.

Whenever you're having a strong emotion—either an unpleasant emotion or a pleasant one—with one corner of your mind, look at the way "I" appears. Observe it. Don't intellectualize about it, saying in an academic voice, "Yes, I feel 'I,' and it appears to be existing within the body and mind but separate from them. Now I understand the object to be negated." In actual fact, you haven't. You're just repeating the words from the text, but you still haven't identified the feeling of "I" in your mind. Don't describe it to yourself with words; rather become familiar with how this "I" appears.

Two Senses of Self

Psychologists talk about people who are co-dependent because they don't have a sense of self. What psychologists mean when they say a person has no sense of self is very different from what the Buddha meant by no-self or selflessness. People with psychological problems actually have a very strong sense of self in the Buddhist sense, although they may not in the psychological sense of the word. Psychologically, they don't see themselves as efficacious individuals in the world, but they still have a very strong sense of "I": "*I* am worthless." When somebody criticizes them, they don't like it. They get into co-dependent relationships to protect or to please this "I." When they fall into self-pity, their sense of an inherently existent "I" is very strong. Thus they still have self-grasping even though they lack a psychologically healthy sense of self.

Buddhism recognizes two kinds of sense of self. There's one sense of self that is healthy and necessary to be efficacious on the path. The object of this sense of self is the conventionally existent "I." The other sense of self grasps at an inherently existent self that never has and never will exist. Within Buddhism, when we talk about realizing emptiness, we're negating the false self, this self that appears inherently existent to us.

In other words, we can realize emptiness and still use the word "I." High-level bodhisattvas (those on the last three grounds) have tremendous self-confidence but no sense of an inherently existent self. They feel, "Yes! I can become a Buddha" and go about creating the causes to do so. Although they have eliminated ignorance, they still have a valid sense of a conventionally existing "I"—the "I" that eats, talks, acts, accumulates karma, experiences its results, and attains enlightenment. Even the Buddha used the word "I" and said, "I talked to so-and-so." So "selflessness" doesn't mean that there's no "I" whatsoever. It means there is no inherently existent person or phenomenon.

When you experience a strong emotion, try to recognize how this inherently existent self appears. Then examine if, in fact, it exists. It appears so vividly, our mind grasps at it so strongly, but does it actually exist? This is something we've never questioned. We've simply assumed that since it appears and since we believe in it, it must exist.

Many things appear to our minds that don't exist at all. When we go to sleep and dream about our latest sweetheart, we really feel that he is there. But, he's not there, is he? That was only an appearance to the mind. Just because something appears to our mind, and just because we believe the appearance, it doesn't mean that thing exists. When we look in the mirror, we see a face. That face looks very real. Is there a face in the mirror? No, there's just an appearance of a face. As babies, we believed it was a real face and tried to play with the baby in the mirror. But the baby in the mirror can't do what a baby does. We may relate to a character in a movie as if he were a person and give advice to him, but there's no person in the screen.

When we take drugs, we see all sorts of things and believe they're there, but they aren't. The same is true with this very concrete "I." We feel it very strongly, but just because we feel it doesn't mean it really exists. So we try to find this "I" that we believe in so strongly, that feels as if it's somewhere inside and related to our body and mind but at the same time is independent from the body and mind. The "I" appears to be in the body and mind but still separate from the body and mind at the same time.

We start checking. We research and see if we can find this "I" that we believe in so strongly. If the "I" exists inherently as it appears to— if it is able to set itself up—there are only two possibilities: the "I" is either inherently one with our body or mind or inherently separate from them. There are no other choices.

We look in our body and in our mind; we look in the collection of the body and mind; we look outside our body and mind. Wherever we look, we can't pinpoint something that is "me." Sometimes we might feel, "I'm my body." If that's so, then who was I when I was a baby? I had a different body then. So am I only my present body? If so, then I didn't exist when I was a baby! If I'm my body, when I say, "I'm daydreaming," does it mean my body is daydreaming because I am my body? But my body can't daydream! It's the mind that daydreams, not the body.

Then we think, "Maybe I'm my mind." Which mind? We have five sense consciousnesses and a mental consciousness. Which consciousness are we? Are we the visual consciousness that sees colors and shapes? The smell, taste, or touch consciousness? Go through each one and ask, "Am I this consciousness?" It's not too hard to see that we're not our sense consciousnesses. Then we think, "Oh, I'm my mental consciousness!" If so, which mental consciousness am I? The angry one? The happy one? The one with faith? The one that's asleep, the one that's awake, the one that meditates? There are so many different moments of mental consciousness. Which one am I? If I'm the present moment of consciousness, who am I when that moment is past? In addition, if I were my mental consciousness, then when I say, "I'm walking down the road," it would mean my mental consciousness is walking. But our mental consciousness can't walk!

We can't find the "I" in our body. Neither one part of our body nor our body as a whole is "me." Neither one mental state nor the continuum of mind is "me." Am I the collection of body and mind? If neither body is "me" nor mind is "me," how can the two together be "me"? If an orange isn't an apple and a grapefruit isn't an apple, how could putting an orange and a grapefruit together make an apple?

Am I separate from my body and mind? Maybe I'm a soul? Something that's going to float up out of my body; maybe that's what I am. My soul. I am separate from my body and mind. My body can die but I remain the same. My mind can be upset but I am not, because I am separate from the body and mind. We have that feeling sometimes, don't we? Is that feeling a valid perception? If the "I" is something separate from the body and mind, my body and mind could be here, and I could be across the room. My body and mind are on this cushion, but I am outside the room. Is that possible?

If I am separate from the body and mind, then I must be able to do something that neither the body nor the mind can do. If so, what? Mind cognizes, body moves. What can the "I" do that neither one of them can do? Whenever we say "I," it is in some way related to either our body or our mind.

Furthermore, if I'm different from mind, then I'm unrelated to mind. So, mind can think, but I'm not thinking. If I'm unrelated to body, then body can hurt, but I won't. Is that possible? Can I think without having a mind that's thinking? When we start to investigate, it's very hard to find an "I" that's separate from and totally unrelated to the body and mind.

Inherently Existent Emotions?

Some people speak about emotions as if they were inherently existent. For example, how does our anger seem to exist? It usually feels very solid: "I am full of rage because of what happened in my childhood." Some people talk as if there were this enormous rage inside them like a volcano ready to erupt at any moment. The rage seems so solid to them, as if they could almost touch it. It seems to be ever-present, and they feel as if they have no choice about what they feel.

But what is rage? How does it exist? Moments of mind arise according to the causes and conditions that are present. When some mind-moments have some similar characteristics, we give them a label such as "rage." That's the only way in which rage or anger exists. Other mind-moments have other similar characteristics and we label that "love." We have both within our mental continuum, but they can't manifest at the same time.

There is no inherently existent anger sitting inside of us ready to explode. When some moments of mind have the similar characteristics of arising in dependence on exaggerating the negative qualities of someone or something or projecting negative qualities that aren't there, finding that object unbearable, and wishing to either harm it or get away from it, we label these moments of mind "anger." That's all anger is. It's a convenient label we use in relation to some mind-moments that are similar. It's not that we're filled with some sort of solid anger. Anger is not who we are. It's not our identity. Meditating on the emptiness of anger like this can be tremendously freeing because we realize that what we call "anger" has no permanent, findable essence. It exists by merely being labeled in dependence on some moments of mind with common characteristics.

Similarly, what we call "compassion" depends on different moments of mind that have the similar characteristic of wishing sentient beings to be free from suffering and its causes. Today we experience some moments of mind that wish sentient beings to be free of suffering. Tomorrow we again experience some similar moments of mind. All these different moments have some connection. The earlier ones contribute to the arising of the later ones. There might be moments of other emotions in between them, but because these moments have some similarities, we label "compassion" in dependence on them. Thus, compassion, which is a part of the evolutionary Buddha-nature, doesn't inherently exist. In fact, both natural and evolutionary Buddha-nature exist by being merely labeled in dependence upon certain characteristics.

Meditating on this is exciting. We get the feeling that things can change because they're not inherently existent. Being empty of inherent or independent existence, things exist dependently. They depend on causes and conditions, parts, and the mind that conceives and labels them. For example, compassion isn't an inherently existent emotion that we either have or don't have. Rather, it arises due to causes and conditions. Therefore, it's possible to cultivate and enhance our compassion by creating the conditions for it to arise. If compassion existed inherently, it would be unchanging; it could not be increased. If compassion existed independently, under its own power, all the compassion we could ever have would be what is there now. Our compassion could never increase no matter what we did. But in reality, as we strengthen the causes and conditions for compassion, it arises more frequently. It's the same with anger. If we cultivate the causes for anger—discontent and judgment, anger will arise more often. Since compassion and anger both exist dependent on causes and conditions, we can choose which one we want to cultivate and go about doing just that.

Lamrim and Deity Yoga

The Chenrezig Yoga Method develops both compassion and wisdom. You'll find that the more compelling your Lamrim meditations on compassion and bodhicitta are, the easier it will be to meditate on Chenrezig, because Chenrezig is the embodiment of compassion. The more in-depth your Lamrim meditations on emptiness are, the easier it will be to meditate on Chenrezig, because Chenrezig is the nature of the wisdom realizing emptiness.

Similarly, the stronger your meditations on Chenrezig—the visualizations, mantra recitation, and so on, the easier it will be to meditate on Lamrim, on compassion, bodhicitta, and emptiness. Lamrim and deity yoga are mutually complementary. Both are necessary. If we just meditate on Chenrezig but don't meditate on Lamrim topics, our compassion may increase by the power of reciting many mantras, but it won't be firm or grounded. If we just meditate on Lamrim without doing Chenrezig, our mind may feel dry. It needs to be softened by purifying and by creating positive potential, and the Chenrezig practice helps in this way. When we meditate on both Lamrim and Chenrezig, these two practices complement each other in a powerful way.

We can do Chenrezig and Lamrim meditation in separate meditation sessions, or we can do them in one meditation session, as Lama Yeshe often encouraged us to do. In this case, we do analytical meditation on a Lamrim topic after we recite mantra. The Lamrim meditation doesn't need to be too long; even ten minutes may have a powerful effect because our mind has been softened by the Chenrezig practice.

According to our need at any particular moment, sometimes we may do more analytical Lamrim meditation on compassion and wisdom, while at other times we may opt to do more Chenrezig yoga. As we observe our mind more, we'll get a sense of what points to emphasize and in what proportion.

By meditating on both Chenrezig and Lamrim, we will understand better what Chenrezig is. When we first become Buddhists, Chenrezig may seem like an external deity. Because we request Chenrezig, "Please, free me from karma. Please be my spiritual guide in all my lives," we may begin to wonder, "It seems just like praying to God. Am I a Buddhist or am I a Christian?"

Such doubts arise because we don't fully understand what Chenrezig is, so we fall back into our old ways of viewing divine beings. Lamrim meditation helps to dispel this confusion and doubt. By meditating on emptiness, we come to understand that Chenrezig is not an independently existent person or an absolute creator. Meditation on karma and compassion clarifies that Chenrezig does not decide what a sentient being's future rebirth will be. By meditating on refuge and the qualities of the Buddha—especially the four bodies of a Buddha, we will understand what a Buddha is and how a Buddha differs from a creator god.

7 *Appearing as Chenrezig*

THE SECOND DEITY:
THE DEITY OF SOUND

"*Within the sphere of emptiness, the aspect of the tone of the mantra* OM MANI PADME HUM *resonates, pervading the realm of space.*" A previous, looser translation of this line reads, "My mind is one with the ultimate nature of Chenrezig's mind, emptiness. This manifests as the sound of the mantra, which pervades all of space. It is as if my mind were sound, the sound of my mind in the aspect of the sound of the mantra, resonating throughout all space."

"*Within the sphere of emptiness*" means that our awareness of emptiness remains. The other five "deities" occur within emptiness. It's not that we meditate on emptiness, but when we begin to generate ourselves as Chenrezig, we forget about emptiness and become an inherently existent Chenrezig. Rather, within emptiness, we become a dependently arising Chenrezig, a Chenrezig that exists by being merely labeled.

Emptiness is a nonaffirming negation. It is a permanent phenomenon in that it does not change moment by moment. The wisdom realizing emptiness is an affirmative phenomenon. It is a consciousness and thus is an impermanent phenomenon that arises due to causes and conditions and changes in each moment. Thus, while the mind is eternal in that it never ceases, it changes moment by moment. In meditative equipoise on emptiness, these two—the subject, mind, and the object, emptiness—become nondual. There is not a sense of a subject—"I" or "my mind"—that is realizing the object, emptiness. The subject, the wisdom realizing emptiness, and the object, emptiness, are experienced nondually in such deep states of meditation.

Furthermore, the ultimate nature of Chenrezig's mind and the ultimate nature of our mind are nondual. Also, we meditate that Chenrezig's wisdom realizing emptiness and our wisdom realizing emptiness become undifferentiable.

At our stage of development, we may not be able to realize emptiness even conceptually, let alone nonconceptually. So when we do this yoga method, we meditate on emptiness and then imagine the experience of nonduality. We meditate on the first deity as best as we are able so that our understanding of emptiness will gradually deepen. Don't get down on yourself if you haven't realized emptiness; if it were easy to realize, we would have become Buddhas by now! If you still have a strong sense of "I" in the middle of the emptiness meditation, don't tell yourself you're a failure. Instead, make use of it in your meditation. Check up on who this "I" is. Is it my body? My mind? The collection of the two? Something unrelated to body and mind? Then, be satisfied with whatever understanding of emptiness you have at that time and try to let go of all preconceptions about yourself. As you practice, your understanding will deepen. So, even if we haven't realized emptiness, at this point in the meditation it is helpful to imagine experiencing nonduality.

When we imagine our mind and Chenrezig's mind becoming inseparable in that both realize the lack of inherent existence, don't get hung up: "Oh, no! Where are you, Chenrezig? I'm supposed to be one with you and I can't find you!" Also, don't be self-critical: "I can't do it right. I'm supposed to be one with Chenrezig, but Chenrezig is blissful and my legs hurt." Just imagine, with whatever understanding you currently have, what it would be like for your mind and Chenrezig's mind to merge in emptiness. Just work with that. It's not going to be a perfect, correct understanding. But we've got to start somewhere, and there's no other way. Slowly, our meditation will develop.

Tantra is like being a little kid and playing dress-up. When we were small children, we put on our parents' clothes and pretended to be grown-ups. We imagined being a firefighter, a nurse, or an astronaut. Before we can actually become something, we have to be able to imagine being it. In tantric practice, we imagine becoming a Buddha like Chenrezig.

One big difference between imagining ourselves as a doctor when we were kids and imagining ourselves as a fully compassionate being in tantra is that in tantra we meditate on emptiness first. Meditation on emptiness is important because everything appears within that state of emptiness, and everything that appears is a manifestation of our wisdom realizing emptiness. While we meditate on the six deities—the different developmental stages in the Chenrezig Yoga Method, we hold the awareness that they are all empty of inherent existence and are in the nature of wisdom.

Lama Yeshe used to ask us, "What is the difference between a mentally ill person thinking he is Napoleon and you thinking you're Chenrezig?" The difference is that the person who thinks he's Napoleon is grasping at a truly existent "I." When we imagine ourselves as Chenrezig, we're not grasping at a truly existent "I." The crazy person thinks there's a real "I" that is a real Napoleon. The meditator knows that neither herself nor the deity inherently exists. That's a big difference. We may not fully understand the difference, but it will become clearer as we practice.

Meditating on the Deity of Sound, the Deity of Letter, and so on is a process of our staying within emptiness while gradually assuming the body of Chenrezig. The sadhana reads, *"Within the sphere of emptiness, the aspect of the tone of the mantra* OM MANI PADME HUM *resonates, pervading the realm of space."* The wisdom realizing the emptiness of yourself and Chenrezig is nondual with that emptiness. That wisdom manifests as the sound OM MANI PADME HUM.

In the first deity, we and all phenomena have dissolved into emptiness, so no conventional phenomena appear. We're not aware of the room, our legs, or the person sitting next to us in the meditation hall. In meditative equipoise on emptiness there's no sense of "I'm sitting here meditating." All that appears to the mind, all that the mind perceives, is the emptiness of inherent existence. Even though we may not have actualized the meditative equipoise that directly realizes emptiness, we imagine that we have. We imagine what it would be like.

Within that emptiness, we start to notice the powerful vibration of OM MANI PADME HUM resonating throughout all space. That vibration, that sound of OM MANI PADME HUM, is our mind realizing emptiness. Don't try to understand this rationally. Just meditate and imagine. Our wisdom realizing emptiness manifests as the sound of the mantra. The sound of the mantra OM MANI PADME HUM is not coming from anywhere outside. There's no pa system out there in the universe broadcasting it. Rather, our wisdom realizing emptiness appears in the aspect of the sound of the mantra, and that mantra sound reverberates throughout all space. That's all there is—just wisdom and compassion in the aspect of the sound of the mantra, filling all of space.

Contemplate this. Take your time. It's a beautiful meditation. Just get in touch with the vibration of OM MANI PADME HUM filling space. Experience that vibration, the pure vibration of your own wisdom mind. It has an incredibly purifying effect. This mantra resonating throughout space permeates everything, even places where there are war and conflict, clinging and repulsion. There's just the sound of this mantra, and its vibration penetrates and purifies everything. In this way, contemplate your wisdom appearing in the aspect of OM MANI PADME HUM, reverberating throughout the universe.

THE THIRD DEITY: THE DEITY OF LETTER

In the first deity, we dissolved into emptiness. Within that, without leaving that awareness of emptiness, our wisdom mind reverberates as the sound of OM MANI PADME HUM. Now, that wisdom mind will appear as the syllables of the mantra that exist within emptiness. As we meditate on the six deities, our wisdom appears in grosser and grosser forms, but still remains intangible and pure.

"The ultimate nature of the deity is inseparable from the transcendental aspect of my own mind." The ultimate nature of the deity is emptiness,

and this is inseparable from the transcendental aspect of my own mind, which is emptiness. This line reminds us that this entire meditation takes place within the emptiness of inherent existence, which is the ultimate nature of both Chenrezig and ourselves.

"This manifests as a moon mandala." Our wisdom realizing emptiness appears as a beautiful, brilliant moon disk. The moon is not spherical but resembles a flat cushion or disk. It's a dazzling disk, completely white, totally pure, radiating right where we were before our flesh-and-blood body dissolved into emptiness. When we meditated on emptiness during the first deity, the appearance of an inherently existent gross body and personality completely vanished. Those don't exist at all. They dissolved into emptiness. When we meditate on emptiness, we cease perceiving erroneous things, such as an inherently existent body or personality.

If there's still some sense of "I" left, which there usually is at our level, don't worry about it. Just remind yourself every so often that everything is empty of inherent existence. Within the empty space, we first experience the reverberation of the mantra and then this brilliant white disk. The moon disk is right in the same place where we were. Above that moon disk is *"the sound of the mantra resonating in space."* The sound of the mantra now *"manifests around the moon in the aspect of written letters, which are like very pure and bright mercury mixing completely with grains of gold."* The sound coalesces to form the syllables of Chenrezig's mantra. These syllables, too, do not exist inherently but are simply an appearance.

A flat, horizontal, transparent moon disk that is made of white light appears where we used to be. Visualize OM in front, MA at about 2 o'clock, NI at 4 o'clock, PAD at 6 o'clock, ME at 8 o'clock, and HUM at 10 o'clock. The syllables are standing upright near the edge of the moon disk. Don't think "I," but if there's some sense of "me," it's as if you're in the center and the syllables OM MANI PADME HUM are around you. The sound, which is your wisdom mind, manifests as the mantra syllables, and the syllables resonate with the sound of the mantra. Each syllable makes its own sound.

Previously, empty space resonating with the sound of the mantra was all that appeared. Now, there's a moon disk with the syllables around us. All of these are the nature of the wisdom realizing emptiness. The syllables are very pure and bright, sparkling like *"bright mercury mixing completely with grains of gold."* That's a really beautiful image, isn't it? Spend some time meditating on these syllables. We can visualize them in Roman letters, in Tibetan script, in Sanskrit—whatever you wish. There they are, and our mindfulness rests on these sparkling, transparent letters. We can't touch them. They are not concrete but are totally transparent. They're an incredibly beautiful appearance, but if we were to reach out and try to touch them, our hand would go right through them.

Our wisdom realizing emptiness manifests as these beautiful, sparkling syllables, and our mind rests on that for a while. Focusing on something pure, such as this visualization, helps our mind tremendously. At first, we may not understand the benefits of this meditation, but imagine for a moment being in a nightclub with a band playing loud music. That sound resonates throughout space, but it gives us an entirely different feeling, doesn't it? That sound is desire-energy or anger-energy and it hooks into the seeds of attachment or hostility within us. These seeds come alive and even the people around us in the nightclub appear to be manifestations of our own desire or hostility. By focusing on them, our attachment and hostility increase even more.

In this meditation, the same process is occurring, but from the unsullied mind of the wisdom realizing emptiness appears the pure sound of the mantra, which then coalesces into the sparkling mantra syllables. Focusing on this, our mind becomes bright and joyful.

THE FOURTH DEITY: THE DEITY OF FORM

In the fourth deity, the Deity of Form, the moon disk and the letters transform into a fragrant, dazzling thousand-petal lotus. The lotus isn't outside us; it *is* us. We're in the middle of the lotus except there's no "I." The lotus is *"glittering with brilliant light. Its center is decorated with* OM

MANI PADME HUM." On top of the lotus is a flat moon with the sylla-bles OM MANI PADME HUM standing clockwise in a circle. It is our wis-dom realizing emptiness appearing as the lotus, moon, and mantra syllables.

"Infinite light radiates from the lotus, moon, and mantra letters, present-ing clouds of offerings to all the Buddhas and bodhisattvas." From the lotus, moon, and the syllables, light goes out in the ten directions—the four cardinal directions, four intermediate directions, up and down. On the tips of the rays of light imagine lovely offering goddesses who present spectacular offerings to all the Buddhas and bodhisattvas throughout infinite space.

These offerings include the traditional eight offering substances: water for drinking, water for washing the feet, flowers, incense, light, perfume, food, and music. We can also offer anything we consider beautiful: cooling ponds, forests with birds, chocolate chip cookies, the latest computers, snow skis, and CDs. Whatever you consider valuable or attractive, offer it to all the Buddhas and bodhisattvas.

Usually we offer the biggest and best to ourselves, and this practice of making offerings to the holy beings challenges this habit. But now we know that miserliness and selfishness cause us suffering, so we hap-pily oppose them by making gorgeous offerings to others. Strange as it may seem, envisioning the offering objects as even bigger and of bet-ter quality than we usually see enables us to realize how transient and unworthy of being clung to they really are.

In general, people don't recognize that Buddhas and bodhisattvas are around them. We don't see them with our eyes, but their minds are omniscient, so their awareness exists throughout infinite space. When we offer these beautiful objects to the Buddhas and bodhisattvas, they're pleased with the offerings. They experience bliss and radiate to us the blessings and inspiration of their body, speech, and mind—that is, all the good qualities of their body, speech, and mind. To know what these are, refer to the refuge section of the Lamrim. Imagine the inspi-ration of those magnificent qualities absorbing back into you, who are at this moment in the form of a lotus, moon, and mantra syllables. As this light absorbs, feel an incredible richness, inspiration, and blessing.

"Again light radiates. On the tip of each ray is the Superior, the Great Compassionate One, going out to purify and empower the sentient beings." "Superior" here means *arya*, somebody who has actualized the path of seeing and has realized emptiness directly. "The Great Compassionate One" refers to Chenrezig. On the tips of all these light rays are Chenrezigs spreading throughout the universe in order to accomplish enlightening deeds. They go to all the various worlds, reaching all sentient beings, not leaving anybody out. Their purpose is to work for the benefit of these sentient beings, to purify and empower them. Imagine Chenrezigs going to your boss, to world leaders, to terrorists, to the poor and the ill, to the arrogant. Send them to Hollywood, the Amazon River, and the stars comprising the Big Dipper—they fill all the universes with their compassionate enlightening activities. These Chenrezigs touch all the sentient beings, relaxing their minds and imbuing them with wisdom and compassion. The light rays purify sentient beings' negativities and banish their ignorance, anger, and attachment.

"A great cloud is emanated and from it a rain of nectar falls, pacifying the sufferings of sentient beings. All sentient beings are satisfied with bliss and become Chenrezig." A great cloud billows forth. From it, nectar rains down onto sentient beings—our parents, friends, enemies, the bully on the playground in grammar school, health care workers, those afflicted with AIDS or with malaria, hell beings, celestial beings, everyone. The nectar pacifies the sufferings of the sentient beings in all the various realms of existence. It extinguishes the fire of the hot hells and heals the painful wounds of the hell beings. The nectar becomes warm rain in the cold hells; it heats them up, gives the beings there light, and soothes their cracked and frozen bodies. The nectar showers on the hungry ghosts, giving them much-needed food and drink. It rains on the demi-gods and gods and pacifies their jealousy and fear at the time of death. It rains on human beings, subduing their restlessness, anxiety, depression, and stubbornness. Everything we've always wished we could do to benefit others we now imagine that these Chenrezigs radiating from our mind do.

"All sentient beings are satisfied with bliss and become Chenrezig." What an amazing thing to imagine—all sentient beings are totally satisfied, they are drenched with bliss and become Chenrezig. Everyone who is ill or dying becomes Chenrezig. The person we just quarreled with becomes Chenrezig. Fleas and mosquitoes become Chenrezig. Little birds and cats become Chenrezig. The Palestinians and the Israelis, the Serbs and the Bosnians, the Americans and al Qaeda—everyone becomes Chenrezig. Imagine all sentient beings are satisfied. They no longer are agitated, discontented, or complaining. The environment becomes a pure land and all sentient beings become Chenrezig.

Relax and have fun with the visualization. It's like the Walt Disney movies we watched as children. Remember cartoons like *Fantasia?* Things radiate out and absorb and transform. We didn't worry about how one bucket of water could become many, or how brooms could sing. Here, too, don't get uptight and try to do it "right." Just enjoy developing your wisdom and compassion through this yoga method. Enjoy extending your noblest aspiration to all sentient beings in all corners of the universe.

Becoming Chenrezig

"All of these Chenrezigs absorb back into my mind, which is in the form of the lotus, moon, and mantra garland." All these Chenrezigs now absorb back into our mind like snow flakes falling into water. This visualization is quite powerful. Then our wisdom mind, which is in the form of the lotus, moon, and mantra syllables, transforms into Chenrezig standing on the lotus and moon disk. We are Chenrezig, white, youthful, radiating, and beautiful. Go through the detailed description of Chenrezig, thinking that this is what you look like.

This meditation challenges our self-concept. Usually we look in the mirror and say, "I have a new pimple. The wrinkles are deeper than before. That mole's getting bigger. My teeth are yellow. That scar on my face is noticeable, and I'm getting a double chin." Reciting a litany of self-criticisms, we put ourselves down. This is what Lama Yeshe used to call "poor-quality view." We never think we look good enough and are never satisfied with our body, our personality, or our spiritual abilities.

Here, we totally transform that. Go through the detailed description of Chenrezig, looking at all the aspects of your Chenrezig body. Everything about us is beautiful. We can't hold on to a negative self-image of being ugly, too fat, or too thin, because now we are Chenrezig. Each aspect of our body is the nature of the wisdom realizing emptiness. Our wisdom realizing emptiness appears in the form of Chenrezig's body. Our mind is still focused on and merged with emptiness, but now it appears in the form of Chenrezig.

Meditating in this way is very profound. A Buddha has two "bodies" or corpuses of qualities—the dharmakaya (truth body) and the rupakaya (form body). To attain these, we have to create the causes: the collection of wisdom, which primarily leads to the dharmakaya, and the collection of positive potential (merit), which primarily leads to the rupakaya. In this meditation, we create these two collections simultaneously, in the same meditation. The mind meditating on emptiness creates the causes for the dharmakaya, and the mind appearing in the form of Thousand-Arm Chenrezig creates the causes for the form body, the rupakaya. In Sutrayana practice, we can't create these two causes simultaneously; they must be accumulated alternately. But a unique quality of tantric practice is this meditation through which the causes for the two Buddha-bodies can be accumulated together.

Our Chenrezig body is made of light. We don't look down and see a roll of fat or skinny ribs. Instead, we have a pure body made of light. Just focus on what it feels like to have a body that looks like Chenrezig, with beautiful, long, narrow eyes looking at everybody compassionately. Imagine being able to look at sentient beings with those kind of eyes. His Holiness the Dalai Lama looks at everybody with an incredible sense of connection, affection, and care. Imagine that you're able to look at everybody in that way, too.

Our dissatisfied, prejudiced, and judgmental mind has vanished. It doesn't exist anywhere because we are Chenrezig, beautiful, radiating light, looking at everyone with infinite, indestructible love and affection. We feel connected to everybody. We're no longer little ol' me whom nobody loves. Instead, our heart is open, and our body language shows that. Chenrezig doesn't sit with his arms folded across his chest. He has a thousand arms reaching out to all sentient beings. Try standing with your arms folded across your chest and see how it feels. Then stretch your arms out. It feels different, doesn't it? The position of our body affects our feelings, and conversely, our feelings are displayed in our body language.

Chenrezig is totally open, totally unafraid. He is free from anxiety and anguish. As Chenrezig, who is empty of inherent existence, we have nothing to defend. We don't need to prove ourselves or protect ourselves from being taken advantage of. We often worry, "If I'm open, I'm vulnerable, and that's frightening. But when I'm afraid, I can't be open," and we get tangled up in our fears. This isn't even an issue for Chenrezig. Chenrezig is just there, with one thousand arms, reaching out to everybody. Chenrezig isn't anxious: "Is somebody going to take advantage of me? Am I vulnerable? Does my best friend really love me?" Chenrezig's body is light; Chenrezig's mind is wisdom and compassion. What's there to be afraid of? Chenrezig doesn't care if somebody likes or doesn't like him, or if somebody praises or blames him. Chenrezig doesn't try to impress others so they will approve of him. Identify completely with Chenrezig. Enjoy feeling like you are the Buddha that you will become. As you do this, psychological machinations fall by the wayside. There's no longer any place for them.

We're so convinced of the self-image that says, "I'm closed because I don't want to be hurt. It's not safe to be open even though I really want to be. I want people to love me, but I can't let their love in because they might leave me or hurt me." We believe these poor-quality self-images. We're sure this is who we are. We make ourselves totally miserable because we're grasping at the existence of someone that doesn't exist. We think that these contorted, low self-esteem images are real, that we are inherently like this. In fact, these images are like rabbit's horns created by our conceptual mind. Rabbit's horns don't exist. Neither does this "poor me" with which we wrongly identify. All the images we have of an inherently existent "I" who is wrong, inferior, helpless, unlovable, cold, and flawed—all these "I"s are rabbit's horns. All these "I"s are totally nonexistent. These self-images are false; such a hopeless, poor-quality me is nonexistent. To help us realize this, we meditated on emptiness before generating ourselves as the deity.

When we realize that such an "I" is nonexistent, the concepts and attitudes grasping at it have nothing to grasp at anymore. Those attitudes evaporate. What are we left with? We're left with just being Chenrezig—empty and compassionate. We don't have to worry about any of that stuff. Give yourself space to imagine what it would be like to go into a room full of people and not to worry about what anyone thinks about you. Visualize yourself as Chenrezig and imagine spontaneous affection arising whenever you see anyone. Imagine what it would feel like to be totally free from thoughts such as, "Am I doing the right thing? Do I fit in?" You're Chenrezig. You naturally relate to everyone in a loving way.

All worry and anxiety are gone. We don't fret about how we look. We aren't concerned with our clothes. "Do my celestial silks match? Are they the right color? Can you see the Calvin Klein label?" There's none of this neurotic self-awareness. We are Chenrezig, and we do what needs to be done. We don't worry about if we're doing it right, if others notice us, if they appreciate us, if we're powerful, if we're successful, if we're important, if we're getting what we want, or if we're safe. All those ridiculous thoughts have evaporated. They no longer exist. Imagine being like that!

You are adorned with three syllables: At your crown chakra, inside your head, four fingers' breadth back from your hairline, there's a very brilliant white OM. Inside your throat chakra is a brilliant red letter AH. At your heart chakra is the brilliant blue letter HUM. These represent, respectively, a Buddha's physical, verbal, and mental faculties. These syllables aren't painted on your skin. The chakras are in the center of your body, in front of the spine.

At your heart is a flat, horizontal, radiant moon disk, with a brilliant white syllable HRIH standing upright on it. In Tibetan, the HRIH has a curve-shaped vowel on top, and you imagine the HUM inside the curlycue of the HRIH. Sometimes they say you imagine the HUM as the principal syllable with the HRIH inside the little dot on the top of the HUM. There are different ways to do it. If you visualize English letters, you can imagine the HRIH being the main syllable with a small blue HUM above it or vice versa. In any case, feel you are Chenrezig, with Chenrezig's body, speech, and mind, and those three syllables bless your three chakras.

Compassion and Wisdom

The basis for doing this practice is compassion for sentient beings. This must be our motivation. Motivated by compassion, we do this practice to increase our compassion. Why? Because we see the kindness of others. We want them to be free of suffering. In addition, we see the value of compassion in our own lives. Having compassion not only benefits other people, it also helps our own mind. When our mind lacks compassion, when we're knotted up and obsessed with ourselves, we're completely miserable. The more our energy is focused on the self in a neurotic way, the more unhappy we are. Paying attention to others, caring about them, and wishing them well become panaceas for our own mind.

Remember times in your life when you were full of affection, understanding, care, and compassion. How did you feel? You weren't depressed, were you? But when we ruminate about ourselves, we're miserable: "Nothing goes the way I want. This person has more opportunities than me. It's not fair." Or "How come no one appreciates me? I always try to please them, but they criticize me in return." This way of thinking produces self-created misery. It's very clear, isn't it?

On the other hand, compassion benefits us and others directly. No disadvantages accrue by having compassion. There's no danger in having compassion. People aren't going to take advantage of us because we're compassionate. If we're stupid, people might take advantage of us, but being stupid and being compassionate are very different. In Buddhist practice, we combine compassion with wisdom, not with stupidity.

Doing the self-generation helps us to develop compassion by imagining ourselves to be the Great Compassionate One. By visualizing ourselves as Chenrezig, we create the cause to become like that. We begin the self-generation process by meditating on emptiness. In the process of doing that, we realize that our ordinary self, as it appears to us, doesn't exist. We see that this flesh-and-bones body that seems inherently existent doesn't exist as it appears. We understand that the personality we cling to doesn't exist the way it appears. As we meditate on emptiness, the appearance of these things as inherently existent vanishes, and we're left simply with awareness of the lack of inherent existence, this nonaffirming negation that is the absence of all the fantasized ways of existence that our mind projects onto people and phenomena.

In Buddhism, we aren't trying to find out who we are; we're trying to find out who we aren't. Our big problem is that we think we know who we are, and we're totally wrong. Our poor-quality view of an inherently existent self isn't who we are. All our judgments and opinions about ourselves create many problems. If we're able to drop these, an incredible spaciousness awaits us. Discovering who we aren't is liberating.

In meditation sessions you might have already experienced bumping up against your self-concepts and preconceptions about how people should treat you, how the world should be, how other people should act or feel, how everything should happen. Working toward realizing emptiness helps us to drop all that. Amazingly, the world goes on just fine—and is even better—without all our "shoulds" being realized.

Summary

To summarize so far: When we meditate on emptiness at the beginning of the self-generation, the appearance of ourselves as an ordinary person totally dissolves. When we meditate on emptiness, there is no conventional appearance at all, especially our ordinary conventional appearance of being poor-quality me with all my problems. Try to stay in that state of emptiness as long as you can. Then, within that, your mind that realizes emptiness starts to vibrate and resonate as the sound of the mantra throughout infinite space. There's just the sound of the mantra. Listen to this pure sound filling the universe.

Then slowly, the sound coalesces, and a moon disk with the syllables OM MANI PADME HUM standing clockwise near its edge appears. Contemplate this for a while.

This then transforms into a lotus and moon with mantra letters. From that, rays of light with offerings radiate to all the Buddhas, and their blessings absorb back into us. Then, we radiate Great Compassionate Ones on the tips of light beams. They pacify the suffering of all sentient beings everywhere.

When you visualize all this, make it personal. Send the light and Buddhas out to everybody: your friends and family, your boss and co-workers, the grocery store clerk, and the income tax collector. They all transform into Chenrezigs and absorb back into your mind, which is in the form of the lotus and moon and mantra letters. Out of that, you appear as Chenrezig standing on a lotus and moon. Then be mindful of what your Chenrezig body made of light looks like: "My center face is white, my right face is green, and my left face is red...I'm holding a rosary, a lotus, and all these other things."

Your arms are stretched out, and your entire body is made of light so nothing hurts. Your beautiful eyes look at sentient beings in all directions. You don't wear colored contacts to make your eyes a nicer color or to see better. The pictures of Chenrezig look flat as if all three heads are facing frontward, but Chenrezig is 3-D, with one face facing frontward and the other two at each side. The palms of our hands have an eye in them. The arms on each side are outstretched from one shoulder, and your hands are soft like lotus petals, even though you don't use hand lotion. There is a white OM at your crown chakra, a red AH in your throat chakra, and a blue HUM in your heart chakra; the Buddha's physical, verbal, and mental faculties are inside of you.

You're wearing attractive, flowing, celestial silks that don't stain when you spill spaghetti sauce on them. You're wearing jewels, which are not heavy like ordinary jewels, and don't need to be insured against theft. These jewels are the six far-reaching attitudes (bodhisattvas' perfections) which adorn us. As Chenrezig, you are naturally beautiful. You don't buy expensive jewelry to make yourself look good or to impress anybody. You don't add something external in an attempt to have self-esteem or to attract others. Instead, as Chenrezig, you are naturally lovely, inside and out. Your body is totally made of light, radiant and transparent, appearing but intangible. Feel, "This is me."

The Fifth Deity: The Deity of Mudra

Here we make the mudra of the lotus essence and touch our heart, brow, neck, and right and left shoulders, as we say, "OM PADMA UD-BHAVAYE SVAHA" five times. This corresponds to the blessing of the senses in other tantras.

8 *Clear Appearance and Divine Identity*

THE SIXTH DEITY: THE DEITY OF SIGN

NOW WE MEDITATE on the deity into which we have generated ourselves. In the long sadhana used during Nyung Nä, after going through the details of the self-generated deity, we invoke the wisdom beings, make offerings to them, and they dissolve into us. Then we invoke the five lords of the Buddha-families, make offerings to them, and receive empowerment from them. Since we are doing a shorter sadhana, these visualizations are not included in the text.

Meditating on ourselves as Chenrezig involves two principal elements:

1. Developing and meditating on the clear appearance of ourselves as the deity
2. Meditating on the divine identity of ourselves as Chenrezig (divine dignity or divine pride).

These two are done to counteract two other elements:

1. Ordinary appearance (the appearance of the ordinary)
2. Ordinary grasping (grasping at the ordinary).

By concentrating on the clear appearance of ourselves having the divine body of Chenrezig, we overcome the ordinary appearance of ourselves as an ordinary samsaric being with an impure body. By identifying with the deity, we overcome conceiving or grasping at ourselves as ordinary beings.

Ordinary appearance has two aspects:

1. The appearance of our ordinary aggregates—a flesh-and-blood body which gets old, sick, and dies, and a mind that is under the control of disturbing emotions and karma
2. The appearance of inherent existence. Our body, mind, and self appear to be inherently existent.

Similarly, ordinary grasping, or grasping at the ordinary, has two aspects:

1. Grasping at or identifying with being little ol' me who's incompetent, unlovable, and stuck in cyclic existence
2. Grasping at ourselves, our body, mind, and all phenomena as being inherently existent.

There's a difference between the appearance of something and the grasping at it. Something may appear ordinary but if we don't grasp at it, there's no problem. When we grasp at it, we're holding that appearance as true. For example, if we look in the mirror, there's the appearance of our face. If we think this is a real face, then we are grasping at a false appearance. But if we don't grasp, hold, or conceive of the face in the mirror to be a real face and recognize it is merely a reflection of a face, we won't be deceived.

Ordinary beings like us not only have the appearance of inherent existence, but also assent to that appearance, thinking, "Yep! That's exactly the way things exist. They exist as they appear to me." Aryas, who have realized emptiness directly, still have the appearance of inherent existence when they are not in meditational equipoise on emptiness, but they don't grasp at this appearance as true. They don't believe it at all. They think, "This is like an illusion. It's like a dream. It appears real but it doesn't exist that way." We can see the difference between appearance and grasping. The appearance of inherent existence is more deeply rooted than the grasping is. The former is a cognitive obscuration—a subtle obscuration that impedes full enlightenment; the latter is an afflicted obscuration—one that impedes liberation from cyclic existence. To become a Buddha, we have to eliminate both of them.

By concentrating on the clear appearance of ourselves as Chenrezig, specifically the clear appearance of our body as being the divine body of Chenrezig, we start to overcome ordinary appearance. By imagining ourselves to be Chenrezig, the appearance of our body, speech, and mind is the appearance of Chenrezig's body, speech, and mind. We don't think that our flesh-and-blood body has become Chenrezig. That body dissolved into emptiness when we meditated on the first deity. Our wisdom realizing emptiness now appears in the form of Chenrezig. It's like we have a whole new body, a body of light in the enlightened form of Chenrezig. When we imagine ourselves as Chenrezig, we think of our body as being wisdom realizing emptiness appearing in that form and focus on the appearance of ourselves as the deity.

To develop and meditate on the clear appearance of yourself as Chenrezig, first do analytical meditation to get a clear appearance of the deity. This is done by contemplating the details of the visualization one by one until we have the image of our whole Chenrezig body. You may start with the feeling of having a body of white light and then focus on the face, until the eyes and other features clearly appear to your mind's eye. Then clarify the details of your Chenrezig torso, your thousand arms, your legs, celestial garments, and ornaments. Be content with the degree of clarity you have and remember it takes time to develop the skill of visualization.

Then do stabilizing meditation on that clear appearance of yourself as the deity to develop concentration. If you can do this on your entire Chenrezig body, very good. But if one part appears clearly and the others don't, focus on that one part for the time being. Later you can develop concentration on the entire body. Concentrate single-pointedly on the appearance of yourself as the deity, using the techniques to develop meditative quiescence (Skt: *shamatha*) as described in the Lamrim and the sutra vehicle. If you don't know these techniques or have forgotten them, study the meditative quiescence chapter in the Lamrim and Kamalashila's texts on meditation. In Kriya (Action) Tantra, using the image of yourself as the deity is one of the objects on which you can cultivate meditative quiescence.

During meditation sessions, spend some time focusing on the appearance of yourself as the deity and developing concentration on that. In Sutrayana, the object of concentration for developing meditative quiescence can be the breath or a visualized image of Shakyamuni Buddha in front of us, among other objects. In tantra, the object on the basis of which we develop meditative quiescence is ourselves as the deity, or perhaps specific seed syllables in different parts of the body. There's a big difference, isn't there? Visualizing the Buddha outside or meditating on the breath doesn't challenge our ego and its multitude of erroneous preconceptions as much as imagining ourselves as a Buddha. In Vajrayana, developing meditative quiescence on our body as a deity's body affects our mind on a very deep level. We're reprogramming the way we appear to ourselves.

Having generated the clear appearance of ourselves as the deity, we then develop divine identity. When our appearance is different, our identity changes as well. By concentrating on the feeling, "I am Chenrezig," we begin to overcome ordinary grasping—the grasping that holds on to a poor-quality image of ourselves and to ourselves as inherently existent. Divine identity counteracts our deluded self-concepts and eventually helps to abolish them.

The "I" that we ordinarily feel to be inherently existent doesn't become Chenrezig because there is no ordinary, inherently existent "I" that exists. It is the "I" that is merely labeled in dependence upon the body and mind that becomes Chenrezig. Through the gradual process of meditating on the six deities, the basis of designation of the label "I"—the body and mind—has been radically transformed. Right now we label "I" in dependence upon an ordinary body and an ordinary mind. In this yoga method, we generate the wisdom realizing emptiness, which is like getting a new mind. That wisdom appears as a body made of radiant light. In dependence upon this body and mind, "I" is labeled. This "I," who is Chenrezig, is not an inherently existent one. It can't be because there is no inherently existent "I" that exists anywhere. This meditation makes that point to us very strongly. The "I" who is Chenrezig is merely labeled; it is a mere appearance, like an illusion.

In this way, meditate on divine identity, the sense of a conventional "I" that exists by being merely designated in dependence on the Chenrezig body and mind appearing to your mind. This divine dignity is the sense of an imputedly existent "I" that is like an illusion, and thus it acts as an antidote to self-grasping ignorance.

This is an incredibly skillful technique for deeply transforming our mind. By meditating on the self-generation, we've totally changed the base in dependence upon which "I" is labeled. Certain aspects of that pure basis of designation are a continuity of the present basis of designation. The continuity of the subtle level of clarity and awareness of our present mind becomes the clarity and awareness of Chenrezig's mind. It's perfectly legitimate to label "I" in dependence upon that mind appearing in the divine form of Chenrezig.

Our mind hasn't realized emptiness yet, but we imagine what that would be like. We don't have Chenrezig's body yet, but we pretend that we do. Using our imagination in this way enables us actually to become Chenrezig in the future. For example, little children dress up in their parents' clothes and pretend to be adults. By imagining themselves as such, they gain the self-confidence to become adults and they also learn some adult behaviors. Similarly, when we're older, we imagine having a certain career. If we can't imagine having that profession, it will be impossible to train for it. When we actually begin training for that career, we develop a new perspective and a different self-image. When we work as interns or apprentices, we keep pretending that we're this new role and rehearse new behavior until finally one day we believe that we are. A similar process is at work here, only we're doing career training to become the Great Compassionate One.

When you reach this part of the sadhana, pause to meditate on clear appearance and divine identity. Although the sadhana doesn't contain many words in this section, this is an important and essential part. If we go through it quickly, thinking that it is insignificant because there are few words in the text, then we have missed one of the purposes of doing the practice.

Spend some time trying to develop meditative quiescence on the clear appearance of yourself as the deity before reciting the mantras. I won't explain these techniques here, but that doesn't mean they're not important. Please study the teachings on meditative quiescence and apply them when meditating on the clear appearance and divine identity of yourself as Chenrezig. Focus your mind single-pointedly on yourself as Chenrezig. When developing divine identity, remember that what is called "I" is merely labeled in dependence upon these pure aggregates, which are the nature of wisdom. Meditate on that for a while.

Then, when you are tired, recite the mantra to rest. "What?," you may ask, "My friends do retreats in which they recite hundreds of thousands of mantra. Isn't mantra recitation the most important activity in the practice?" Because we beginners are unable to concentrate for very long, we may meditate on clear appearance and divine identity briefly and then go on to mantra recitation. By reciting many mantras with an attitude of faith in the Chenrezig Yoga Method and by doing our best to meditate on Chenrezig, we create a lot of positive potential. This strengthens our mind so that as more seasoned practitioners, we will be able to meditate for long periods of time on clear appearance and divine identity, which are more important elements of the sadhana than is mantra recitation.

The Inseparability of the Two Truths

While visualizing ourselves as Chenrezig, we also contemplate the inseparability of the two truths, conventional and ultimate. The special techniques of tantra enable a practitioner to develop an awareness of both conventional truths, the level of appearance, and ultimate truths, the deeper mode of existence—that is, emptiness.

Only a Buddha can perceive the two truths simultaneously. Until then, at any particular moment all other beings are able to perceive either conventional truths or ultimate truths, but not both simultaneously. In Sutrayana, we meditate on the two truths separately, for example, meditating on bodhicitta at one moment and meditating on emptiness in another. An arya following only the Sutrayana who is in meditative equipoise on emptiness cannot simultaneously perceive conventional truths. Nor can she perceive emptiness directly while perceiving conventionalities after she arises from meditative equipoise.

In the lower tantras, of which this Chenrezig practice is one, one aim is to generate one consciousness that can perceive the two truths simultaneously. Practices of Highest Yoga Tantra have more techniques to do this. Going from Sutrayana to the lower tantras to Highest Yoga Tantra is like going from one step on a staircase to another, higher one.

While visualizing ourselves as Chenrezig (conventional truth), we remember that we (Chenrezig) are empty of inherent existence (ultimate truth). We are not a truly existent Chenrezig. The truly existent "I" dissolved into emptiness at the time of the first deity. Within this lack of inherent existence, the pure aggregates of a deity arose. In dependence on these, the label "Chenrezig" was given and Chenrezig appears. Since our mind is so familiar with grasping at true existence, at this point we meditate that "I" as Chenrezig is empty of inherent existence. Thus while appearing, Chenrezig is empty, and while being empty, Chenrezig appears. This meditation on the union of the two truths prevents us from falling to either of the two extremes—absolutism or nihilism. Absolutism is the extreme of reification, that is, grasping at inherent existence; while nihilism is the extreme of denigration, for that view believes that phenomena are totally nonexistent. In other words, an absolutist view holds that if phenomena exist, they must inherently exist, and a nihilistic view holds that if phenomena are empty of inherent existence, they must be totally nonexistent. Both of these views are incorrect, and are therefore called extreme views.

Sometimes, while visualizing ourselves as Chenrezig, we fall to the extreme of thinking Chenrezig is inherently existent. That's natural, because our habit from beginningless time has been to see everything as inherently existent. Inherent existence appears to us, and we grasp it as correct. It's easy to do, even when we generate ourselves as Chenrezig. We feel, "Now I'm inherently existent Chenrezig." To counteract this, while imagining ourselves as Chenrezig, we remember that Chenrezig is empty of inherent existence. We reflect on the emptiness of the deity to free ourselves from any tendency to grasp at inherent existence.

Other times, when we meditate on emptiness, our mind goes to the extreme of nihilism, thinking, "In emptiness there is no appearance of conventional phenomena, so nothing exists at all." This extreme is very dangerous, for if we believe in it, we will negate cause and effect, karma and its results. To counteract this, we meditate, "While Chenrezig is empty, Chenrezig also appears."

In the extreme of absolutism, we hold things as inherently existent. In the extreme of nihilism, we negate things and think they don't exist. We tend to go back and forth between these two extremes because our grasping at inherent existence is so strong. We think, "If they aren't inherently existent, then they're totally nonexistent. If they do exist, then they must be inherently existent." Both of these are inaccurate. We get to the Middle Way view by remembering Chenrezig appears but is empty; Chenrezig is empty but appears. In other words, the two truths exist harmoniously. They complement each other, and in fact they depend on each other.

Meditate on emptiness: Because the pure aggregates of Chenrezig and the "I" labeled in dependence on them are merely labeled, they don't exist from their own side. They're not there within the basis of designation. Anything that is merely labeled in dependence upon a base doesn't exist within that base. When you meditate on that, you may have a feeling of spaciousness.

If you begin to fall to the extreme of nihilism, think, "Chenrezig is not empty of all existence whatsoever. Chenrezig appears, like an illusion." Try to see these two truths at the same time. Try to understand that something can appear and also be empty, and that its ultimate nature must be empty in order for it to exist and appear conventionally.

Every phenomenon, even emptiness itself, is empty and exists conventionally.

Meditating on Chenrezig's emptiness counteracts self-grasping ignorance, which is the root of cyclic existence and the chief of the afflicted obscurations that prevent liberation. However, even someone who has perceived emptiness directly still has the appearance of inherent existence, which is a cognitive obscuration, which prevents full enlightenment, when she arises from her meditation. Until the state when someone is a Buddha, there's always the mistaken appearance of inherent existence except when she is in meditative equipoise on emptiness. Aryas and arhats don't grasp that appearance as true, and instead see it as like an illusion. We, on the other hand, grasp the appearance of inherent existence as being the way things are, and this is the source of all our problems.

Meditating on Chenrezig appearing but being empty brings home the point that the appearance of inherent existence is false. As beginners, we do this on the level of imagination. It's very good training for us, for it helps us to see that the two truths exist simultaneously and do not harm each other. Philosophically speaking, we say the two truths are the same nature but are nominally different. Meditation on the inseparability of the two truths helps us see how dependent arising and emptiness come to the same point and complement each other.

In Kriya (Action) Tantra, to which this Chenrezig practice belongs, a practitioner develops the wisdom of clarity and profundity. Clarity is imagining having the body of the deity and identifying with it: that is, having clear appearance and divine identity. Profundity is the wisdom that knows that the deity's body and the "I" are both empty of inherent existence. Clarity corresponds to the dependently arising nature, and profundity corresponds to the empty nature.

Things are dependent in three ways:

1. They depend on causes and conditions
2. They depend on their parts
3. They depend on the mind that conceives and labels them.

We can meditate on any or all of these three ways of dependency when we visualize ourselves as Chenrezig.

By meditating on clarity and profundity together, we develop method and wisdom. Method focuses more on dependent arising and helps us relate to conventional truths properly. Wisdom focuses on the empty nature and enables us to perceive the ultimate truth. In Tantrayana, we try to unify these two in one consciousness. This is quite a profound meditation, and there's a lot to think about here. As you hear and contemplate teachings on bodhicitta and emptiness, bring those understandings into this practice.

Meditate on clarity and profundity in this way when you're not reciting the mantra. When you get tired and need to relax, recite the mantra. Or if your mind is restless, do some mantra recitation, calm your mind down, and then come back and do more silent meditation on the topics we just covered. We have to know how to work with our mind—when to recite the mantra, when not to recite it, how to balance the two, and in which order to do them.

Mindfulness

Many people speak of mindfulness these days and the word seems to be used in a variety of contexts. Some Theravada practitioners describe mindfulness as nonjudgmentally observing what it going on in the mind. Others use it to mean holding in mind what is valuable to practice, and this meaning concords more with how the term is used in Tibetan Buddhism. There we find mindfulness described as a mental factor essential for the attainment of meditative quiescence, for it remembers the object of meditation in such a way that we do not become distracted by other objects. Mindfulness is also important in the practice of ethical discipline, because this mental factor remembers our precepts, what to practice, and what to abandon.

Zopa Rinpoche taught mindfulness when instructing us on walking meditation: "As you walk, ask yourself, 'Who is walking?' Your body? Your mind? The collection of the two? An 'I' that is separate from the body and mind? Be mindful that you say, 'I am walking' simply because the body is walking. There is no findable 'I' that is walking aside from what is merely labeled. Be mindful of this." Here we see that the word "mindfulness" does not refer to observing or noting what is occurring in our mind—that is more the function of the mental factor, vigilance —but to mean holding in mind the dependently arising and empty nature of phenomena.

Its usage in tantric practice is similar: remembering or holding in mind the object of meditation and the factors to cultivate during this meditation. We practice mindfulness as we meditate on each of the six deities, first being mindful of our empty nature, then of the sound of the mantra reverberating throughout space, and so on, until the Deity of Sign. Throughout this entire process, it's especially important to remain mindful that the dependently arising evolution as Chenrezig occurs within the sphere of emptiness.

When we meditate before saying the mantra, mindfulness focuses on the clear appearance of ourselves as Chenrezig and of the divine identity of being Chenrezig. The more mindful we are of being Chenrezig, the harder it is for disturbing emotions and negative thoughts to arise. This mindfulness is a strong factor to change our self-image.

Furthermore, we remain mindful of clarity and profundity. Initially, we go back and forth between the two understandings: Chenrezig appears but is empty; Chenrezig is empty but appears. We are mindful of dependent arising and of emptiness. As our meditation deepens, we unify these two understandings, and mindfulness is placed on the complementary nature of the two truths. Thus we see that mindfulness in a tantric context pulls us out of ordinary appearance and ordinary grasping and introduces us to the qualities of an enlightened mind in a profound way.

Changing Our Self-image

While meditating on clarity and profundity, sometimes we think, "I'm not really Chenrezig. Why am I sitting here pretending to be some guy with a thousand arms? This is stupid." When we had such doubts, Lama Yeshe used to reply, "You believe you are all your negative self-images. I think that's pretty dumb." When asked about taking drugs, Lama said, "You don't need drugs to hallucinate, dear. You're hallucinating all the time. You're hallucinating an inherently existent, ordinary you. You're hallucinating an inherently existent, ordinary world and beings around you. Dharma is to help you stop hallucinating!"

This meditation strikes very deeply at our self-image. Meditating that we're Chenrezig and sending out light and visualizing being of benefit to all sentient beings is counter to our usual way of thinking of ourselves. Sometimes doubt arises, and we fall back into our old self-image: "I'm sitting here imagining radiating light. I can't radiate light! I'm such a jerk. I can't do anything right! I don't have a beautiful body made of light. My body is this dumpy old thing that stinks!" We constantly fall back into our old image and believe it is real. This is why Lama said, "You're not who you think you are. Why are you grasping at that image, so sure that's who you are? That's not who you are."

We bump into this old image all the time when we're trying to develop the appearance and identity of ourselves as the deity. We have to examine that poor-quality self-image and question why we believe in it so much. We rarely doubt the heaps of images we've dumped on ourselves. One layer of self-concept—grasping at a truly existent "I"—is innate and has come from our previous lives; it is the innate self-grasping ignorance that has obscured our mindstream since beginningless time. Other layers of self-concept have been acquired in this life: "I am this nationality, this socioeconomic class, this educational level, this ethnic group, this gender, this religion, this sexual preference, this profession, this age. I like this and don't like that." We're so sure this is who we are. This causes a lot of problems in our life, especially when somebody else doesn't agree with our self-image. Then we get really upset: "I think I'm a pretty nice person but this person thinks I'm incompetent, and that one thinks I'm ugly, and this one thinks this, and that one thinks that." We can get really mad when others don't agree with our self-image, when they think we're less than we think we are.

Likewise, we get upset when people have a better image of us than we have of ourselves. When people genuinely praise our good qualities, sometimes we feel embarrassed: "Hey, wait a minute. I'm not that good." Sometimes people love us, and we think they're all wrong for doing so: "If you only knew me, you wouldn't love me. You must be dumb if you care about someone like me."

Often I hear Dharma students say, "My teacher pushes me." Actually, our teachers aren't pushing us. They have more confidence in us than we have in ourselves. Our teachers look at us and see somebody who can become a Buddha. They see somebody who has so much potential. But we look at ourselves and say, "I can't do that." As a result of our limited self-image, we think, "My teacher expects too much of me. I'm hopeless. I can't develop the determination to be free. I can't develop bodhicitta. My teacher expects me to become a Buddha. But I can't become a Buddha. I'm too dumb!" Of course our teachers think we can become Buddhas. If they didn't think that, they wouldn't teach us the path to Buddhahood. But they don't expect us to become Buddhas overnight. They aren't going to get mad or judge us if we don't. Nevertheless, they see potential in us that we can't yet see.

The practice of divine identity hits hard at our lack of self-esteem and our beliefs that hold, "I can't practice the Dharma. I have so much attachment that there's no way I can change." Or, "I'm so full of anger I can't generate bodhicitta. These practices are wonderful, and I admire them, but I just can't do them. This is useless, so why is my teacher pushing me so hard?" Sometimes we become defensive like this, misunderstanding our teacher's encouragement and confidence in us to be pushing us to do things we don't think we can do.

In the early '70s, I taught third grade in the Los Angeles city schools. A little boy named Tyrone was in my class. Tyrone had the self-image that he could not learn to read. But he was smart, and I knew he could learn to read if he tried. But because he didn't believe he could learn, he didn't try, and as a result, he didn't learn to read very well. It was sad.

We construct so many identities. These are all creations of our mind, but we believe they are reality. With a poor-quality self-image, we put ourselves in prison. That's why this yoga method is so powerful: it shakes up that identity. It helps us to see that we have a lot more potential than we think we have, and that our teacher's confidence in us isn't misplaced.

In Dharamsala, I went to see Ribur Rinpoche, a gentle, old lama from Tibet. I told him my dream of starting a monastery in the United States. He said, "That's an excellent idea. You must do it. Very good idea." And then I began to tell him all the reasons why I couldn't: "There aren't so many senior monastics, and they are scattered in many countries. There isn't any money, and there's not a place to live. No other senior nun wants to help—they're all busy—and I can't do it alone." He looked at me and said, "You just make up your mind and do it!" I just stood there dumbfounded. What he was saying seemed impossible to me. But he planted the seed, and years later I was able to found Sravasti Abbey (by some miracle or maybe due to Chenrezig's blessings).

His Holiness the Dalai Lama constantly says that all sentient beings have Buddha-nature, but we think, "Not me! I'm hopeless. See if he can make me into a Buddha!" Doing this meditation enables us to begin to shed some of those layers of identity. We develop courage and willingness to take risks and try new behaviors. This yoga method begins to give us confidence to try at an imaginative level to act like a Buddha. We begin to get the feeling that we're capable of doing a Buddha's activities.

Here's an example of how we get twisted up in our self-image. Many years ago, I was teaching a course at Tushita in Dharamsala and was responsible for eighty participants. While the course was going on, Zopa Rinpoche had a few older students come to his room at 4:15 in the morning to do *Lama Chöpa*. I was the only one of them involved in the course. After *Lama Chöpa*, I would lead the morning meditation and teach most of the day.

Needless to say, toward the end of the course I was a little short on sleep. One night Rinpoche was going to do Yamantaka self-initiation and invited the senior students to his room to do it. When we do self-initiation, we renew our tantric vows. So I thought, "Wow! I need to renew my tantric vows. And it's so great meditating with Rinpoche." Besides, everybody else was going and I didn't want to be the only kid on the block who was left out. I thought, "Rinpoche will want me to be there to renew my tantric vows, and if I don't show up, what will he think? He will know how lazy I am."

But inside me, there was civil war: "I'm so exhausted. I have to get up early and teach the people in the course tomorrow morning. If I go, I'm not going to be able to do that."

I was hard on myself: "Go, Chodron. You've got to renew your tantric vows because you've broken them so many times. If you really had compassion for sentient beings, you would go."

"But, I'm so tired," I lamented to myself. Back and forth I went, at war within myself. Neither side of me had much compassion for the other.

In the end, I decided not to go so that I would have the energy to teach the next day. I went to sleep feeling guilty and telling myself what a lousy Dharma practitioner I was, how lazy I was, how I was missing this excellent opportunity to renew my tantric vows. I worried about what Rinpoche was going to think of me: "I'm such a bad student. If I only had more bodhicitta, I would overcome my laziness and go. Rinpoche stays up all night. That's because he has compassion for all sentient beings. But look at me. I'm such a pathetic wreck. I have to sleep because I don't have enough compassion to work diligently for the sake of sentient beings. Why can't I do it right?"

The next day, I felt rotten about myself. But I was able to teach the students at the course and lead the meditation sessions because I'd slept. Later in the day, I went to see Rinpoche and confessed, "Rinpoche, I'm really sorry I didn't go to self-initiation last night." I was so concerned about what he thought about me. I wanted him to forgive me.

"What?" he said.

"Rinpoche, I feel so guilty. I didn't go to the self-initiation. I'm really lazy."

He said, "Please get me that," and pointed to something across the room. I got it and then tried to bring the subject back to my not going to the self-initiation, but he completely refused to engage me on this topic. He ignored my saying how guilty I felt, what a poor practitioner I was, how lazy and selfish I was.

I kept saying it again and again, and he didn't respond to it. Eventually, I got it. He didn't even think it was important enough to talk about. It made me stop and think. Clearly, he didn't have the same image of me that I had of myself. I was certain Rinpoche thought of me what I thought of myself: "I'm lazy. I'm a failure. I don't practice hard enough, blah, blah, blah." I was sure he had that image of me because that's who I am. He must see that. But, he didn't have that image of me at all. It was a very good lesson. I had to look at myself and say, "Why am I hanging on to all this stuff and beating myself up? For Rinpoche what I did is a nonissue."

The point here is to question our self-image. We have many self-images that we don't even recognize as self-images. We're completely convinced that that's who we are. When we visualize ourselves as Chenrezig and hold that divine identity, we begin to recognize how many layers of inaccurate self-concepts we have. To counteract them, we remember that the "I" is empty of having any inherent identity. Within that emptiness, we generate ourselves as Chenrezig. This practice gives us the mental space to be somebody else after we dissolve that ordinary "me" into emptiness. We realize that the ordinary person, that inherently existent, awful person that we're sure we are, doesn't exist at all.

Then, we get in touch with our own wisdom, which manifests as the deity. We have to identify with our wisdom mind instead of with our garbage mind. We identify with Chenrezig, who radiates compassionate light to everyone, who can be completely equanimous no matter who he's with, who doesn't have to correct everyone. We start developing a new identity.

After meditating on the six deities and generating yourself as Chenrezig, spend some time in silent meditation, meditating on clear appearance and developing meditative quiescence on that clear appearance.

Then, meditate on divine identity. Stay with the feeling, "I have Chenrezig's capabilities. I can have equal, open-hearted affection for everyone. I don't have to lose my temper." It's especially effective when cultivating divine identity to think about situations that we find difficult: "I'm Chenrezig. I can go to this family gathering and be happy. I don't have to have all my buttons pushed by my family. I can go and be Chenrezig and radiate light. They may criticize or disagree with me, but I don't have to get angry. I'm Chenrezig. Chenrezig doesn't get angry when people put him down. Chenrezig doesn't catch the ball when they throw it. He just lets the ball go by. I can, too. I can let those comments go by. I don't have to react to them. Anyway, those comments are about that ordinary person, and that ordinary me doesn't exist. It's just a false self-image. I'm Chenrezig now. I don't have to be trapped by who I think I am."

People in families often push each other's buttons. But now, when we practice being Chenrezig, we think, "I don't have any buttons to be pushed, and I'm not going to push anybody else's buttons. I don't have to antagonize them or pick on them in order to defend myself. I don't have to have the last word. I don't have to prove to them that I'm right, successful, or competent. As Chenrezig, there's no ego to defend so I don't act that way."

By meditating like this, our minds become habituated to a different way of being. There's some mental space to be creative with how we act in situations in which previously we would have become defensive, judgmental, or aggressive. Now we can go into them and be happy, relaxed, and beneficial to other people.

Meditating like this is practical. When we know we will meet a difficult person or be in an awkward situation, that morning we imagine being Chenrezig in that situation. We imagine someone criticizing, ridiculing, or putting us down, except we don't react the same old way because we don't identify with our former, deluded self. Now we identify with Chenrezig's compassion and wisdom and react as an enlightened being would. As *The Thirty-seven Practices of Bodhisattvas* prescribes:

Even if someone broadcasts all kinds of unpleasant remarks
About you throughout the three thousand worlds,
In return, with a loving mind,
Speak of his good qualities—
    This is the practice of bodhisattvas.

Though someone may deride and speak bad words
About you in a public gathering,
Looking on him as a spiritual teacher,
Bow to him with respect—
    This is the practice of bodhisattvas.

Even if a person for whom you've cared
Like your own child regards you as an enemy,
Cherish him especially, like a mother
Does her child who is stricken by sickness—
    This is the practice of bodhisattvas.

When we have the divine identity of being Chenrezig, we try thinking and acting in this way. We may surprise ourselves and be able to do it!

Two Ways to Please Sentient Beings

A bodhisattva's or a Buddha's behavior is said to be very pleasing. But what does that mean? There are two ways of pleasing others, one which accords with the Dharma, the other which doesn't. Pleasing others because we genuinely care about them, without expecting gifts, love, praise, or other ego gratification in return, accords with the Dharma. Pleasing others because we want them to like us, to not be mad at us, or to give us praise or gifts is worldly action. Such behavior may look kind, but in fact it is self-centered. Because we have many expectations, the relationship gets sticky and complicated and generally leads to disappointment.

We may think, "A good Buddhist is a people-pleaser." That is incorrect. Of course, Buddhas try to please sentient beings, alleviating their suffering and bringing them temporal happiness. In addition, Buddhas look at the bigger picture, which includes not just the temporal happiness found in cyclic existence, but the happiness of liberation and enlightenment. In particular, they want to please sentient beings by leading them to enlightenment. To do that, sentient beings may have to experience some discomfort. Buddhas don't care if sentient beings like them, approve of them, or speak well about them in the short term. They care about the welfare of sentient beings in the long term. This is similar to a doctor who wants to cure a person with a horrible disease. He may prescribe some foul-tasting medicine that the patient complains about taking, but the doctor doesn't care if the patient complains or criticizes him because his concern is the other's long-term welfare.

Benefiting others is possible when we have an altruistic intention. When we're a people-pleaser, we won't do anything that people don't like even if it's ultimately for their benefit. We're too attached to what they think about us. In an effort to win their approval, appreciation, or love, we try to do only the things that please them. This motivation leads to a dead end. Why? First, it's impossible to please sentient beings. Sentient beings are in samsara, so they have dissatisfied minds. They always want more and better. Secondly, pleasing others so that they'll like us is deceptive; we're acting like a phony and in the long run both we and others will suffer from our trying to pretend to be something we aren't. We don't have to try to win others' approval and love. If we train ourselves to have a good heart and a kind motivation, others will be attracted to us. Even if they aren't, it doesn't disturb our inner peace.

Similarly, it's impossible for others to please us. There's no way for them to meet all our needs or for us to meet all of theirs. As sentient beings, we always think, "If someone would only do x, y, z, then I'd be happy." Someone does it, and then we find something else we want or something else to complain about. Our minds are so fickle!

When we try to please other people, we get tied up in knots: "Am I good enough? Do they like me? Am I meeting their needs?" It becomes all about "me." However, when we identify with Chenrezig, we work for the long-term benefit of sentient beings, which is the best benefit to offer them.

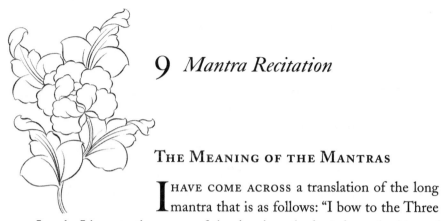

9 *Mantra Recitation*

The Meaning of the Mantras

I HAVE COME ACROSS a translation of the long mantra that is as follows: "I bow to the Three Jewels. I bow to the ocean of the Arya's exalted wisdom, the king of marvelous manifestations of Vairochana, the one thus gone, the foe destroyer, the perfectly complete Buddha. I bow to all the ones thus gone, the foe destroyers, the perfectly complete Buddhas. I bow to Arya Avalokiteshvara, the bodhisattva, the great being, the great compassionate one. It is thus: OM, (you) will hold, will hold; do hold, do hold; hold, hold! (I) request power; move, move! Thoroughly move, thoroughly move! (You) hold a flower, hold an offering flower; method and wisdom, supreme guru; burned with mind, may it be removed; arrange it!"

I have not been able to check the accuracy of the above translation, nor have I heard an extensive explanation of its meaning. Nevertheless, it gives an idea of Chenrezig's wonderful qualities and abilities.

The translation of OM MANI PADME HUM is easier, although its meaning is very profound. OM represents Chenrezig's body, speech, and mind, which is what we want to attain. MANI means "jewel" and indicates the method, or compassion, side of the path. PADME means "lotus" and refers to the wisdom side of the path. All realizations of both the sutra path and the tantra path are included in these two words. MANI also refers to dependent arising and PADME to emptiness. These two express all existents: conventional truths and ultimate truths. HUM refers to the Buddha's mind, which we want our mind to become.

When we recite these two mantras, we are calling out to great compassion unified with wisdom appearing in the form of Chenrezig, expressing our aspiration to actualize these two wondrous qualities in our minds. Contemplating the meaning of the mantras as well as doing the visualizations make mantra recitation most meaningful. But even the simple recitation of the mantra has benefit. I remember Lama Yeshe telling us, insistently, "Even if you don't want to develop compassion, recitation of OM MANI PADME HUM will make compassion grow in your mind." I believe this occurs because of the effect of the vibration of the mantra in our subtle body and mind. This is my thought, but it's better if you check it with your own experience.

Usually when we think about doing a retreat on a specific deity, reciting a certain number of mantras comes to mind. In fact, meditating on the clear appearance and divine identity of ourselves as the deity is more important, and we should stop and meditate on these. The texts recommend reciting mantra to refresh ourselves when we need a break after meditating on clear appearance and divine identity. For us beginners, however, spiritual mentors often recommend reciting a certain number of mantras because that is easier for us. It also gives us a sense of accomplishment when we succeed in doing that.

The sadhana contains many visualizations and meditations to do in different proportions depending on our level of practice. Beginners are unable to meditate very long on clear appearance and divine identity. We do those for a short time and then go on to the mantra recitation because that's more active and helps us to focus better. As we progress, the balance changes. Great yogis probably don't say a lot of mantra. They focus on the heart of the meditation—the meditation on emptiness in the first deity, the meditation on clear appearance and divine identity, the meditation on clarity and profundity, and other meditations which will be discussed later.

While reciting the two mantras, we maintain the appearance and identity of Chenrezig. At our heart chakra, inside our chest and in front of the spine, is an open lotus flower. On the lotus is a radiant flat moon disk. The lotus and moon are horizontal and are made of light. At the center of the moon the syllable HRIH, the essence of Chenrezig's mind of wisdom and compassion, stands upright. Forming a circle around the HRIH, starting in front and going clockwise, are the syllables OM MANI PADME HUM. Outside of that, closer to the edge of the moon, are the syllables of the long mantra, NAMO RATNA TRAYAYA ..., also standing clockwise in a circle. The letters are radiant, made of light, glowing and sparkling.

PURIFYING SENTIENT BEINGS

"Light radiates from these (the HRIH and mantra syllables) and completely fills my body. All obscurations, diseases, and hindrances are purified." We begin by purifying and transforming ourselves. Let the light fill you, let yourself feel unencumbered by disturbing attitudes and negative emotions. Any areas of your body that are painful or diseased are filled with healing light and all tension leaves your body. Enjoy this feeling of relaxation and freedom.

"The light radiates outside, carrying a countless number of Great Compassionate Ones. They purify all sentient beings' negative karma, disturbing attitudes, negative emotions, and obscurations." Now the blissful light, with a Chenrezig on the tip of each ray, streams out of you and touches each and every sentient being—those whom you like, those whom you don't, and those you don't know. When this glowing light touches each sentient being, it performs two functions: it purifies them of their negativities, and it inspires them to realize all the stages of the path to enlightenment. We may start imagining the light touching the beings in the room and gradually spreading out to those in the area, the country, the continent, the world, and the universe. Or we can start with our friends and family, then radiate light to strangers, and finally to those who have harmed us or of whom we're afraid. Or, we can first radiate light to human beings, then animals, hungry ghosts, hell beings, demi-gods, and gods. We can use our creativity and imagination when doing this visualization. Each meditation session can have a different emphasis.

It's very easy to love sentient beings in a general way. But it's more effective to be specific in our visualizations. Send light to the guy who cut you off on the highway. Send light to the IRS employee who questioned your tax return. Send light to the terrorist who thinks that killing others in the name of God will cause him to be reborn in heaven. Send light to government leaders who think that bombing others solves problems. Send light to your teenager who leaves his room a mess and gets mad when you comment on it. Send light to specific people you know and care about, people who are having problems, strangers, and people you don't like. Send it to hospitals, the Middle East, the inner cities, and Beverly Hills. There's suffering everywhere.

The light frees sentient beings from their suffering. This doesn't mean just the "ouch" kind of suffering, but all the types of *dukkha* (unsatisfactory conditions)—the *dukkha* of pain, the *dukkha* of change, and pervasive compounded *dukkha*. Take some time to reflect on the meaning of the three types of *dukkha* and how much sentient beings are oppressed by them. Send light to the beings suffering from all those kinds of *dukkha*. You may want to imagine sending light to each of the six realms individually and stopping the particular sufferings in each. The light becomes rain that extinguishes the fires in hell and transforms all the hell realm guardians into nurses who then care for the hell beings' wounds.

Send light to the beings in the cold hells, where it lights up and heats the environment. The light becomes warm energy that helps those beings recover from what they have gone through. If you find it easier, think of the hells as a mental realm, as beings with great mental suffering. For us who grew up in wealthy countries, that may be easier to imagine because in our lives we probably have experienced far greater mental anguish than physical pain. Still, I think it's helpful to see the various realms as more than mental states; certainly the human and animal realms are. Thus, other realms may be so as well.

Send light to the hungry ghosts, beings with enormous stomachs and thin necks. Think of the hungry ghost mentality and how that manifests in our society. Aren't various types of addiction—to drugs, alcohol, shopping, sex, and gambling—the hungry ghosts' mentality? Whether one has a human or a hungry ghost body, the mind grasps strongly at external pleasures but experiences only frustration and dissatisfaction in the process.

Send light to all the beings who suffer as animals. Think of the animals who are slaughtered and chopped up. Think of those shot for sport or trapped in fishnets. Send light to the ones sprayed by chemicals, the ones eaten by other animals, and those exploited for their labor, fur, skins, and other body parts. Send light to calm and transform their pain. Think of the suffering of pets—they may have comfortable homes and lots of food, but they cannot think clearly or practice the Dharma. I try to teach my cats about the first precept, not to kill, but they don't understand. While they're comfortable in this life, they still experience *dukkha* because they don't have the fortune to have a body and mind that are serviceable for Dharma practice.

Send light to all the human beings so they can resolve the predicaments they get themselves into. If you know someone who just died, imagine that person in front of you, and think the light purifies all his negative karma and inspires his mindstream with good qualities. Similarly, send light to anyone who is dying, sick, grieving, or experiencing mental torture.

You can begin by sending light to the people sitting around you. It's easy for us to ignore those near us and yet think, "I'm sending light to all the sentient beings." Connect with the people around you instead of ignoring or skipping over them. Think of all the *dukkha* they experience in cyclic existence and send the light of your compassion to eliminate it.

Send light to the beings in the asura, or demi-god, realm. These beings suffer tremendously from jealousy. As the legend tells, Mount Meru is at the center of this world system. It has eight levels; the four upper levels are inhabited by the desire realm gods, and the four lower levels by the demi-gods. In the god realm, beautiful trees with delicious fruit abound. The roots of these trees are in the demi-god realms, inciting jealousy in the demi-gods: "The roots are here so we should have the fruit," they say. The gods reply, "Too bad, the fruit's on our land, and you can't have any." The demi-gods are so jealous that they begin a war with the gods. It's a sad situation, and unfortunately something akin to it happens in our world, only instead of fighting about fruit, we struggle to gain oil.

Send light to the gods, those beings with so much sense pleasure that they're totally distracted from practicing the Dharma. They indulge their craving continuously and are totally absorbed in pleasure. However, just before they die, they become aware that it is all going to end. Their gorgeous bodies begin to stink and their friends desert them. The suffering they experience at this time is unbelievable. The day at Disneyland is over, and they're overwhelmed with agony because they must separate from it and know they will be reborn in a worse place.

We can see the six realms as different life forms or as states of mind. Meditating on beings in the hell realms helps us to think about anger and its effects and inspires us to counteract it. Considering beings in the hungry ghost realm prompts us to think about miserliness and makes us want to be generous instead. Thinking of beings in the animal realm enables us to reflect on the effects of ignorance and to counteract it. Enlightening the beings in the demi-god realm makes us consider the disadvantages of jealousy and to let it go, and sending light to the beings in the god realms reminds us not to be obsessed by pleasure.

In this way we remember to restrain ourselves from actions that cause rebirth in those realms and actions motivated by those negative emotions. Visualizing purifying the six realms and stopping the sufferings of the beings there also helps us to generate genuine love and compassion. By focusing on others' experiences, we eliminate the pain of our self-centeredness. When we just think about our own problems, we suffocate. Here, by sending light to the beings of the various realms, our attention is on others, and compassion for them arises. Compassion frees us from the pain of self-preoccupation.

Keep sending light and transforming all the beings of the six realms. If you want to do this in a detailed way, you can give sentient beings the things they need to solve their gross suffering. Then, when they are more comfortable, send them Dharma teachers, Dharma books, and a community to practice with. Imagine they practice the teachings, gradually developing all the realizations of the path until they become Chenrezig. This is a joyful meditation because we imagine others actualizing their Buddha potential. They are no longer trapped by the afflictions in their minds or by the suffering in their external circumstances. Instead they become fully enlightened Buddhas.

Our mind has a hard time holding the image of all beings as Chenrezig and very easily slips back into thinking they are ordinary. So, keep doing this practice, continually transforming them, not because they need it, but because we forget that they have become Chenrezig and start thinking of them again in an ordinary way. Furthermore, purifying, inspiring, and enlightening them again and again makes our love, compassion, and resolve to benefit them firmer. It increases the power of our bodhicitta.

PRACTICING GENEROSITY

"The light gives sentient beings all the temporal happiness they want." This is similar to the giving part of the taking and giving (*tong-len*) meditation. The light becomes everything sentient beings want and need. Give washing machines to those who need washing machines. Give medicine to those who are ill. Give Dharma teachers to the sentient beings who want to listen to the Dharma. Send homeless people food, shelter, new clothes, companionship, job training, and a job. Send visitors and friends to those who are isolated and lonely. Imagine whatever sentient beings need being conveyed to them on the tips of the light rays emanating from the HRIH and mantra syllables at your heart. Imagine them being satisfied and happy, and rejoice at their happiness.

This meditation prompts deeper questioning within us: "What do sentient beings actually need? What does it mean to help someone?" If somebody is homeless, sending them food and a place to live is a good start, but it isn't sufficient to solve the problem. We also have to send them skill in managing their finances, job training, tips for job interviews, self-confidence, and so forth. We need to teach them how to get along with others and to resolve conflicts. However, even with all these, they are still subject to being born and reborn in cyclic existence under the influence of afflictions and karma. Thus we have to send them Dharma teachers and teachings presented according to their disposition, so that they can transform their minds and attain liberation and enlightenment. While sending light to various people, contemplate deeply, "What do they need in the short term? In the long term? How can I help them use what they receive so that they are able to bring about happiness in their lives?" Reflecting on what it means to help others expands our mind, so that instead of having "idiot compassion," we will have skillful compassion backed by wisdom. Then, when we encounter those who need our help, we'll have a better idea of how to help them.

"It (the light) also ripens their minds so that they receive the realizations of the gradual path to enlightenment and attain the ultimate happiness of Buddhahood. All sentient beings become Chenrezig." Here we imagine sending sentient beings all the proper conditions to practice the Dharma. Each country has different conducive circumstances that people need in order to learn. In places such as China and Tibet, people need freedom of speech and freedom to follow their religion. Imagine sending that to them. In Cambodia, send them a peaceful country. In the West, send qualified Dharma teachers and pure teachings as well as translators and Dharma teachers who speak the local language. This encourages us to consider deeply, "What are conducive circumstances for Dharma practice? How do we create them?"

A circumstance that is conducive for growth for one person may not be so for another. For example, when I lived in Nepal, I was happy to stay at Kopan Monastery and do my practice. I didn't want to go to Kathmandu to do the shopping or to run errands for the monastery. There was one monk who liked to go to town to do that, and I was glad that he did. But I wonder if our respective conditions were really conducive for our growth. Somebody like me, who loved formal practice and disliked going to town, needed to learn to be more active in serving sentient beings. The monk, who loved to be active and had a hard time sitting on the cushion, needed to do more sitting meditation. Doing what we like or what we're good at may not always be the best thing for us.

A good teacher refines the Dharma instructions according to the mentality of each particular student. They tell one to do the shopping and one to do Nyung Nä, and that is the right advice for both of them. Ajahn Chah, a Thai Theravadin master, explained that if someone is walking on a path with precipices on both sides, we tell someone who is too close to the right side, "Go left!," while we call out to someone who is near the left side, "Go right!" If we hear the advice apart from the circumstance in which it's given, it sounds contradictory. However, understood properly we see that it is consistent.

In *The Four Hundred Stanzas*, Aryadeva says that if a disciple has great attachment, the teacher should have him work serving sentient beings. But if the disciple has a lot of anger, the teacher should be very nice to her and let her have her way a little bit so that she can calm down. If we treat a person with attachment the same way we treat a person with anger, that person may develop more attachment, which isn't helpful for his practice. If a person with anger is pushed and challenged in the same way a disciple with attachment should be, her anger may increase. She needs a calmer situation so she can look within and work on her anger.

Thinking about these things during our meditation helps us to develop skillful means for handling our own emotions. In addition, we become more compassionate and sensitive so that we can help sentient beings in appropriate ways. All these meditations help us to develop our wisdom, compassion, and skillful means. In them, we rehearse being Chenrezig, who has developed these three qualities to their fullest extent. Cultivating these qualities is a gradual process. We don't go from zero to complete perfection instantly. We must patiently and persistently train our mind through meditations such as this one.

Once we've given sentient beings conducive circumstances for Dharma practice, we imagine them realizing the path to enlightenment. If we don't have much time, we imagine that they quickly realize the path and attain Buddhahood. However, it's more effective if we think of leading them gradually along the path because that's how it's actually done. We've got to stick with sentient beings and not give up on them no matter how many mistakes they make or how disgusting their behavior is. We've got to hang in there in order to teach and lead them gradually. This is how Chenrezig and our spiritual mentors guide us. They haven't given up on us, and we aren't angels! No matter how obnoxious we disciples are, they keep teaching and guiding us. So we should develop the fortitude to do that for others.

Thus we imagine teaching sentient beings the gradual path to enlightenment, step-by-step. To do this, we have to be familiar with and meditate on these same steps. So while reciting the mantra, we may think about each Lamrim topic, develop an understanding of it in our own mind, and then imagine, as Chenrezig, explaining it to others. This is an excellent way to clarify and increase our own understanding of the Lamrim. First, think about how to listen and teach the Dharma properly; then give sentient beings the ability to hear the teachings in a proper way. Next, think about how to rely on a spiritual mentor. When your understanding of that is clear, explain it to others and imagine the light rays give them the realization of this topic. Continue with precious human life, its usefulness and its rarity, and explain these meditations to sentient beings; then go on to impermanence and death, and so on, up to and including the path of tantra.

In this way, go step-by-step through the entire gradual path. Generate an understanding of each meditation, and send that experience to all sentient beings. In this way, do the giving part of the taking and giving meditation while meditating on the entire Lamrim. Don't just intellectually say, "I give them the realization of emptiness." We have to get some feeling of emptiness and then send that to them.

Meditating in this way is very effective for integrating the Lamrim into our minds. We think about the Lamrim at the same time that we say mantra, which helps the mind to focus. After reaching a conclusion from the Lamrim meditation, we send that understanding to sentient beings.

Sometimes we focus on one Lamrim topic each meditation session. Other times, we may want to do a glance meditation that covers all the essential topics while reciting mantra. Think briefly instead of extensively about each topic, and send the light out, giving all sentient beings those realizations.

Another possibility is to go through each far-reaching attitude (perfection) one by one, thinking about each subcategory in it—for example, the three types of generosity, the three types of ethical discipline, and so on. Think about its meaning and send that to all sentient beings. Imagine that they generate that same realization in their minds. In this way, sentient beings become Buddhas.

Visualize sending billions of manifestations to all corners of the universe. These touch sentient beings, giving them what they need, bringing them happiness, and leading them on the path to enlightenment. By visualizing in this way, we generate confidence that we can actually do this. Mother Teresa, for example, couldn't have done what she did if she didn't have self-confidence. We may look at what she did and say, "I can't do that." But we're exactly the same. We both have Buddhanature. It's just a matter of how we look at ourselves. If we have the confidence to do something, we have taken a big step in being able to do it. This meditation method gives us the confidence to start acting like a Buddha. How does a Buddha act? Without ego, without self-centeredness. A Buddha is totally fearless and compassionate.

While reciting the mantra, we can also do the taking and giving meditation. As Chenrezig, imagine taking on all the sufferings of sentient beings. While we inhale them, they transform into a thunderbolt that destroys any residual afflictions, self-preoccupation, or cognitive obscurations in us. Then, as Chenrezig, we radiate light to all the other sentient beings, transforming our Chenrezig bodies and becoming the beings that sentient beings need to meet, transforming our Chenrezig possessions and giving sentient beings the things they need, and transforming our Chenrezig merit (positive potential) and giving sentient beings conducive circumstances for practice and the realizations of the gradual path to enlightenment.

Another visualization is to emanate millions of Chenrezigs from our heart. They go to rest on top of the heads of all sentient beings. Light flows from those Chenrezigs into every sentient being. This is similar to the visualization that we did before, but the Chenrezigs on everyone's head emanated from us. We and all sentient beings say the mantra together, purifying the five afflictions and transforming them into the five pure wisdoms.

These are some suggested visualizations. It's not necessary to do them all in each meditation session. Some sessions we may emphasize one, other sessions we may do more than one. Knowing many different ways to meditate enables us to maintain interest in the practice by varying the visualization when needed.

MAKING OFFERINGS AND RECEIVING INSPIRATION

As we continue reciting the mantra, we visualize, *"Again, light rays radiate from my heart. They carry offerings to all the Buddhas and to all the sentient beings who have become Chenrezig. All these Chenrezigs are extremely pleased and experience bliss."* From the HRIH at our heart, offering goddesses emanate in all directions. They present beautiful offerings to all the Chenrezigs in space, as well as to all the sentient beings who have been transformed into Chenrezig.

The purpose of offering is to accumulate positive potential (merit), counteract miserliness, and cultivate delight in giving. We can offer whatever we consider beautiful. In ancient India, a host would offer a respected guest eight offerings—water for drinking, water for washing dust from the feet, flowers, incense, light, perfume, food, and music. These became the eight offerings that are given in a sadhana.

Illustrations of these offerings are put on the altar before we begin the practice, one row beginning from the deity's right (our left as we face the altar), which is offered to the front Chenrezig, and another row starting from our right that is offered to the self-generation. We can update the offerings, and we should offer things we like. For example, I think Chenrezig would like chocolate chip cookies much more than *tormas*—Tibetan ritual "cakes" made from barley flour—so I offer these on the altar.

While reciting the mantra, offer other things you enjoy—beautiful, unpolluted hiking trails, forests, and ponds. The goddesses also offer things you're attached to, such as the latest model computer or the newest digital equipment. If you like, offer flashy motorcycles, SUVs, goddesses with pierced tongues and tattoos, and Game Boys. Of course, by the time this commentary is published, these will all be old-fashioned and something new will be in! Offer whatever you consider beautiful to all these Chenrezigs. Multiply the offerings and make them more beautiful, so these wondrous objects fill the entire sky. With a happy mind, offer them to all the Chenrezigs, who experience bliss when they receive them.

"Then all the qualities of Chenrezig's holy body, speech, and mind in the form of white light come from all the Chenrezigs and absorb into my heart, blessing my mind. All the Buddhas and all the sentient beings who have become Chenrezigs fall like snowflakes into me. I feel very blissful and my body, speech, and mind become inseparable from Guru Chenrezig's holy body, speech, and mind." Here, imagine limitless Chenrezigs falling and melting into you like snowflakes melt into a lake. Concentrate on receiving their blessings, inspiration, and realizations. At this point, contemplate very strongly what it would feel like to actually be Chenrezig. We are completely filled with infinite Chenrezigs, and our body, speech, and mind are inseparable from those of Chenrezig. Imagine how this would feel.

All these Chenrezigs melting into us makes our body completely at ease. If there are any aches or pains, the light and nectar go right there, filling that area with bliss. So many joyful, compassionate Chenrezigs fill that space. Any sickness or pain and the negative karma and obscurations that cause them come out from our lower orifices in the form of disgusting substances, just like in the Vajrasattva sadhana. Alternately, think that it all disappears completely, just as turning on a light instantly dispels the darkness in a room. Feel free of all disease, contamination, pollution, interference from other living beings, and negative karma. Feel free from all anxiety, fear, depression, and self-doubt.

As these Chenrezigs dissolve into you, let go of your dysfunctional physical, verbal, and emotional habits. These include such things as sleeping or eating too much, complaining, correcting everyone, despair, and worry. Infinite Chenrezigs melt into you, purifying the four karmic results of past actions. It's important to think and feel, "That negative karma has now been purified." This involves forgiving ourselves. We have to let go of a negative self-image that believes, "I'm such a jerk because I did this and that twenty years ago." As the Chenrezigs flow into us, think, "I made that mistake before, and now it's purified. I've learned from my mistake and don't feel guilty or ashamed." Or think, "Now that habit is finished. I don't have to act that way anymore. I can act differently."

To summarize, while reciting the mantras, we contemplate that as Chenrezig we radiate light to others, which purifies and enlightens them. We make offerings to all the Buddhas and all the sentient beings who have become Chenrezig. They then absorb into us, infusing us with bliss. This presents a different idea of what it means to be inter-dependent with the things in our universe. In Chenrezig's universe, external things dissolve into us, and we emanate beautiful things into the external universe. The separation that we usually feel between "me" in here and the rest of the world out there diminishes; we experience interconnectedness, enjoying the flowing nature of relationship.

Sometimes it may seem that there is too much to do and to think about while reciting mantra. Do we focus on the visualization? On the sound and vibration of the mantra? On the meaning of the mantra? On generating compassion? On applying the antidotes to whatever dis-turbing emotions arise and distract us? We may become confused because we aren't able to do them all at once, and that confusion becomes yet another distraction. Then we criticize ourselves for getting confused. Pretty soon, a circus of silly thoughts is spinning in our head, making us unnecessarily miserable.

As we practice, we learn to work effectively with our mind. Each meditation session is different, and we learn how to sense what will keep our mind focused on a virtuous topic at any particular time. Sometimes the visualization will be primary with the sound of the mantra in the background. Among the various visualizations, one session our mind may be primarily attracted to making offerings; in another session it may go naturally to enlightening sentient beings or to experiencing all the Chenrezigs absorbing into us and blessing us. Other times, the sound of the mantra is our primary object of focus.

If an emotion or thought arises while we're meditating, we notice it and bring our concentration back to the mantra or visualization. However, if it is forceful and our mind keeps returning to that worry, grudge, or daydream, we temporarily turn our focus to applying the antidote to it. Once that issue has been worked out, we return to the visualization and mantra recitation.

You can recite as many of the long and short mantras as you wish during a meditation session. Some days you may wish to recite more of the long mantra, other days the short mantra may automatically arise within you. At the conclusion of reciting the two Chenrezig mantras, recite the Padmasattva mantra three times to purify any mistakes you may have made in doing the sadhana, reciting the mantra, or meditating on Chenrezig. Padmasattva is white and looks like Vajrasattva. He is called Padmasattva and the mantra is slightly different from the Vajrasattva because Chenrezig belongs to the Padma family, whose head is Amitabha Buddha.

10 *Working with Our Stuff*

THE VIBRATION of the mantra affects our body and mind. Reciting mantra has a purifying effect that we can feel physically and mentally. It doesn't occur immediately, but gradually the energy of the mantra begins to work and calms our mind. However, a stormy period often precedes the pacification of the mind. The pure vibration of the mantra brings out our impure energy, confusion, and other traits that we would rather not look at. We would much rather present ourselves as well-balanced, competent, and confident people, even when we don't feel that way inside. When our "garbage mind"—as Lama Yeshe used to call it—spills out, we may be alarmed and think that we're not doing the practice correctly. In fact, we are. Only by exposing the garbage mind can we identify it and free ourselves from it.

Before Mount St. Helens, a volcano in the northwest U.S., exploded in the 1980s, it looked great on the outside—it was lofty, snow covered, and magnificent. Meanwhile, below the surface magma was building up. Similarly, we look great on the outside, but inside there's volcanic activity, rumbling, and bits of steam sneaking out: "I'm fine. My life's together. I know what I'm doing. I've got to look like a good Dharma practitioner. People shouldn't see me cry. They shouldn't know how distracted I am during meditation. I can't let on how incredibly confused I am." We think we're the only one who is confused and not wanting to lose face, we hide our turmoil and pretend to be calmly in charge of the show. But we're in cyclic existence, so how much control do we really have? How peaceful can we be when we have a samsaric body and mind?

When we meditate and recite mantra, our façade begins to crack, revealing what is really going on in our mind and heart. Attachment, hostility, jealousy, arrogance, vengeance, craving, shame, fear, guilt, and anxiety are starkly apparent. At this time, we shouldn't wallow in these emotions or become depressed because we have them. Getting discouraged isn't the purpose of meditation. There's no reason for the Buddha to have spent forty-five years teaching the Dharma if his goal was for us to be depressed. We can do that all by ourselves.

It's very good when our garbage mind comes up, because then we have a chance to work with it, clear it out, and apply the antidote to counteract or transform it. Don't think that you're doing something wrong when negative emotions surface. Observe them arising, and then apply the thought training teachings to counteract them. The trick is not to get involved in the story behind the emotions. If we do, the emotion will feel very solid. Instead, watch the thoughts that form the story behind the emotion and ask yourself, "Are they true?"

For example, let's say I'm trying to meditate on Chenrezig and the thought, "My friend betrayed my trust" pops into my mind. If I'm not aware, before long I will be either hurt or angry, depending upon my usual pattern of reacting to such thoughts. I'll review the details of the story I've thought about many times before: "My friends did x, y, z when I trusted them. Then they did a, b, c." We might then think, "I was so stupid for trusting them. It's all my fault," or "Who do they think they are treating me like that!," or "How could someone do this? What did I do to deserve such treatment?" And away we go. We become screenwriters for the melodrama in our mind. Who is the star of this film? *Me*, of course.

If we are able to catch this process early on and do not get involved in it, we find it amusing. If we catch it later, after our mind has already bought into the story, we have to apply the antidote. In this case, it's helpful to contemplate verse 6 of *The Eight Verses of Thought Transformation*. We see that we had false expectations that we communicated.

Or perhaps they were communicated, but the other person is an imperfect living being, just like us, and thus wasn't able to fulfill them. We contemplate that our karma got us into that situation: in the past we have betrayed others' trust and now a similar experience is happening to us. In this way, feelings of hurt and anger fade away.

Another way to counteract negative emotions is to practice divine identity as an antidote. If you start to get self-critical, depressed, or discouraged, remember that you're Chenrezig. Give yourself another way to look at the situation besides the old pattern, the one that you've used before that doesn't work. Instead, identify yourself as Chenrezig and ask yourself, "How would Chenrezig look at the situation?"

Sometimes we'll remember a situation that happened ten, twenty, or even thirty or more years ago. If that happens, go into that situation, except this time be Chenrezig. Be there with your family, or whoever it was, and be Chenrezig. As Chenrezig, radiate light from the HRIH at your heart. The light fills the whole room and touches all the people around you. It purifies them, relaxes their minds, and transforms them into Chenrezig. They and we are now Chenrezig, so who will be angry, upset, or disappointed in whom?

Visualizing this is very effective, for it shows us an alternative way to view the situation and to act besides falling into our old, dysfunctional emotional patterns of fear, defensiveness, resentment, inferiority, helplessness, defiance, clinging, or insecurity.

Each time this memory comes to mind, we become Chenrezig and imagine purifying everyone who was in that situation that happened years ago. Each time a habitual emotional pattern arises, we imagine being Chenrezig and imagine reacting the way an enlightened being would react to those circumstances. We do this again and again, each time deepening our understanding of the Dharma and healing the remnants of the past that we carry around with us in our minds. We can meditate like this while chanting the mantra.

A disturbing attitude and emotion will arise in cycles. After we work on it using the Dharma, it probably won't come up as strongly for a while. It might come up a month later, a year later, or the next time we do retreat, but that time we'll be able to identify it more quickly and see more clearly how it is based on distorted perception. Some of these issues won't disappear completely until we attain the path of seeing. We need to be patient and to continue to peel off the layers.

Be enthusiastic about examining the state of your mind and working with it. In some sessions, the mind will be very clear, and you'll be able to focus on clear appearance and divine identity for a long time. In other sessions, the mind will be restless, and hurt feelings, anger, or jealousy will arise. At other times, the mind will go wild with craving and desire. At these times, it's helpful to say the mantra, do the various visualizations, and meditate on Lamrim and thought training to help pacify and let go of whatever has come up. Each session will be different as you incorporate into your meditation whatever is going on in your life and mind. When the mind is overwhelmed by afflictions, be creative and find skillful ways to use the Chenrezig meditation to work with them.

Try to recognize when your mind is off track and apply Dharma antidotes right away. This helps enormously. The more we work with these emotions in our meditation, the more we will be able to let go when they arise in our daily life. In similar situations in the future, our attitude will be different because we've practiced developing new ones.

Although this meditation stretches our ordinary image of ourselves, we may still keep bumping into it. We sit on our cushion, recite mantra, radiate light to all the sentient beings, and it's so wonderful. We feel great. It's so easy to love sentient beings and watch compassionate light flow to them, except for certain sentient beings, such as your boss who criticized you, the neighbor who irritates you, the drunk who swore at you, or the financial consultant who mismanaged your retirement fund. Then we get stuck. We can radiate light to all the sentient beings except to this person. In the middle of our very nice meditation we think of that person and suddenly we stop being Chenrezig. We fall back into our old image of ourselves as little ol' me who has to defend myself against this person I can't stand.

When you bump into things like this, try to work with it. Don't run away, ignore it, or get mad at yourself. Instead, gently investigate, "Why can I radiate light to everybody but this person? What is my button that gets pushed in regards to them?" Notice the question is not, "How can they possibly do that?" or "Why are they so neurotic?" The question is about us: "What are my buttons? Why do I get upset, feel threatened, become insecure? What inside me finds their action or words unbearable?" Exploring this, we learn about ourselves. We apply thought training and Lamrim teachings to work with these emotional hurdles. Slowly, we'll work our way through them and will be able to extend compassion and radiate light to that person, too.

SELF-RIGHTEOUSNESS AND THE JUDGMENTAL MIND

Sometimes, just watching the news creates agitation and anger in our mind. Self-righteous feelings and judgment arise because "those idiots" are doing something we don't like. Work with that self-righteous, judgmental mind in your meditation. Others may do negative actions, but why do we need to be contemptuously "holier than thou" in our response? Why can't we cultivate a compassionate response to others' negativity? After all, they're confused about what causes happiness and what causes suffering, and they're under the control of mental afflictions which harm them. Thinking in this way enables us to have compassion, because we see that others don't mean to harm us when they act in certain ways. Then we can send light and purify other sentient beings of their negative karma.

Someone once asked Lama Yeshe whether Mao Tse-tung was an evil being. His army killed many people and due to his actions, many people, including Lama himself, were adversely affected. Lama looked at us and said, "He meant well, dear." We were waiting for Lama to make a strong political statement, especially since he had to flee Tibet due to Mao's army, carrying only his tea cup with him, and enter India as a refugee. We were a group of liberal Westerners, ready to scream "injustice" on behalf of oppressed people, but Lama just said, "He meant well, dear."

Often, people act harmfully but think they're doing something good. Their minds are overwhelmed by disturbing attitudes and karma. I'm sure we can look at our own past and see things we've done and say, "How could I have done that?" Looking back and understanding our own mind, we see that we were overwhelmed by afflictions and karma. We weren't a horrible person who meant harm. We were just totally confused at that time. Understanding this, we forgive ourselves and, in doing so, become less judgmental and more forgiving of others.

I'm not saying that we should just sit on our cushion and radiate love in response to oppression, poverty, and violence. We need to engage and try to solve the problems in the world, but we should do so with a positive attitude, not with a mind full of despair or anger.

Before or after watching the news, do the Chenrezig meditation and send light out to purify all those sentient beings. Try to figure out which afflictions are motivating them to do what they're doing, and imagine the light purifying specifically those disturbing attitudes and negative emotions. Think about the kind of karma those people are creating and what kind of results that karma could bring. Ask yourself, "What did they do in the past to make this behavior habitual so that they're still doing it now?" Then, send light to them to purify the seeds of past actions that cause this habitual behavior and to cleanse the karma they're creating now so that they don't have to experience future suffering.

Preferences and Opinions

Our preferences and opinions arise while we meditate and can be great distractions. Often we don't realize them as the attachments and views that they are. Instead we mentally dig in our heels and insist that our way is right. For example, my teacher, Zopa Rinpoche, likes to begin teaching in the evening and go into the wee hours of the morning. I, however, am a morning person and don't like staying up late. Sometimes, I become agitated when teachings begin late and have lots of "good" reasons to support why they should begin early: "I practice during the day and am tired. If I go to bed late, I'll sleep late, and that interferes with my morning meditation. Plus, when teachings begin in the evening, I fall asleep during them, and that's disrespectful to my spiritual teacher and to the Buddha." Don't you think these are good reasons to teach early in the day, not late at night? I think they're excellent reasons! And probably some other students in the room agree with me. But are these the absolute truths that they appear to be when my mind is agitated? No, they are simply my preferences, and the more I cling onto them the more I suffer.

Having received the novice, or sramanerika, ordination in the Tibetan tradition in 1977, I went to Taiwan in 1986 to receive the full ordination for women and become a bhikshuni. During the one-month training program that surrounded the ordination ceremony, all five hundred of us trainees had to file into the main hall and immediately file out of it into the teaching room each morning. To my efficient mind, this was a waste of time; I had a much better plan about how everyone could arrive in the teaching room. Did the ordaining masters care about my plan? Not at all, not to mention the fact that I couldn't make it known to them because we spoke different languages and that it was out of place for me as a trainee to tell the masters what to do. So for a month I had to bear this inefficiency and waste of time. It was only later that I realized that my agitation was due to attachment to my own preferred way of doing things. It was I who was wasting my time by dwelling on "my way is the right way."

There are many ways to bring distractions into our meditation so that we work with issues pertinent to our lives. Sometimes we do this by thought training. For example, instead of fighting the situation, we accept that the principal cause is our previous destructive actions. This gives us courage not to follow our self-centeredness and negative emotions in the future. Sometimes we can transform that person into Chenrezig and then see how we feel about him. Try to cultivate pure appearance of him instead of seeing him as ordinary. Instead of labeling "Sam" in dependence on that person's ordinary aggregates, label "Sam" in dependence on their Buddha-nature. Imagine Sam becomes Chenrezig, and then relate to Sam as if he were Chenrezig.

When you are Chenrezig radiating healing and inspiring light to others, don't think of sentient beings as an amorphous group. Instead think of specific people. Transform each of them individually into Chenrezig. Try to recognize that they each have Buddha-nature and develop an attitude of equanimity toward them all. Try to see that they're all empty of inherent existence. Sam has not always been the same Sam with a cut-and-dried fixed personality. In the previous life he wasn't Sam, and in the future life he won't be Sam either. One day he will be a Buddha.

GUILT AND SHAME

When we meditate, things from the past come up, and we have to work with them. We may remember times when we treated others horribly—hurting their feelings, deceiving them, repaying their kindness with spite, manipulating them, cheating them. While regret for these actions is appropriate and necessary to purify these karmas, we often fall into guilt and shame instead. Guilt and shame are obstacles to overcome on the path, because they keep us trapped in our self-centered melodrama entitled "How Bad I Am." Regret, on the other hand, realizes that we erred, leads us to purify, and motivates us to refrain from acting like that in the future.

How do we counteract guilt and shame? One way is to recognize that the person who did that action no longer exists. You are different now. Is the person who did that action five years ago the same person you are now? If she were exactly the same person, you would still be doing the same action. The present "you" exists in a continuum from that person, but is not exactly the same as her. Look back at the person you were with compassion. You can understand the suffering and confusion she was experiencing that made her act in that way.

A second antidote is to do the taking and giving meditation, thinking, "I will take on the suffering of everybody who did this same horrible action that I did. I will take on the pain of all the victims of these actions." In this way develop compassion and use it to dissolve the self-centered feeling that says, "I am the worst, the most unforgivable one."

Another method is to focus on the purification visualization before doing the self-generation as Chenrezig. Imagine that light and nectar stream into you, purifying that negative karma, as well as your guilt and shame. Think that Chenrezig forgives you. A voice inside may say, "Chenrezig, what I did was so terrible, how can you forgive me!" Be careful! That comes close to criticizing a Buddha, doesn't it? It's like you're saying Chenrezig does not know what he is doing when he has compassion for you.

Another way is to meditate on emptiness. The object to be negated is the solid, real "I" who did such a horrible thing five years ago. Search and try to find that "I." Determine that it either has to be in the body and mind or separate from the body and mind. Start looking: Am I my body? Am I my mind? Search everywhere for this disgusting person you think you are. Finally, the understanding will dawn that you can't find that person because he or she doesn't exist. No such inherently existent person is to be found anywhere.

Sometimes you may feel, "I cannot find the solid 'I,' but there is still this feeling of 'I.' So the feeling must be 'I.'" Is the feeling or the thought "me" the "I"? Is a thought a person? Is a feeling a person? If I think of a grapefruit, is my thought of a grapefruit a grapefruit? There is a thought or feeling of "I," but that is not me; that is just a thought, a feeling. When you try to find the one that is me, it's like trying to catch a rainbow.

Dharma isn't separate from our daily life. Bring these meditations into your life and use them to solve your problems. Above are some examples of how to do this. Be creative in your own meditations and discover other ways to soothe and dispel your disturbing emotions.

THE FOUR PURITIES

During the self-generation meditation, we imagine the four purities, which are attributes of Chenrezig—pure body, pure environment, pure activity, and pure enjoyments. This meditation brings many benefits: by imagining being Chenrezig with these four purities, we create the cause for that to occur. By holding these four in our minds during break time, we counter our ordinary appearance and grasping, thus transforming everyone and everything into circumstances conducive for enlightenment. In addition, overcoming aversion becomes easier because we think of everyone and everything as being a pure attribute of Chenrezig.

The purity of body is generating ourselves as Chenrezig through the process of the six deities and holding the clear appearance and divine identity of ourselves as Chenrezig. We've already talked about how this challenges the "poor me" view. Because we imagine having a body made of light, this meditation counteracts our attachment to our ordinary body and our aversion to it not being as attractive, strong, or healthy as we would like.

The purity of environment involves imagining our environment as pure, instead of viewing it as the ordinary environment we're always dissatisfied with. To do this, we send light to the toxic waste dump, to the garbage fills, to the nuclear testing grounds, and to oceans covered with oily foam. We send the light wherever it is needed to purify the environment and imagine it becoming a pure land where everything is conducive for Dharma practice.

It's not sufficient to visualize our environment being a pure land, we must actively stop polluting it and start cleaning it up. Lots of us talk about "*those* people who pump pollutants into the water and air," but we have to examine how much we contribute to this. For example, do we carpool or do we drive somewhere alone so we can come and go when we want? Do we arrange our errands so that we drive the minimum possible? Or do we get in the car and take a drive because it feels good and we want to see something different?

I see so many plastic forks, paper plates, and styrofoam cups at Buddhist centers. We talk a lot about interdependence and compassion, but do we actively change our consumer lifestyle and simplify? Do we wear clothes and shoes until they are worn out or give them to a charity if they are still in good condition? Do we recycle our paper, newspaper, plastic bottles, glass, and cans? One time I had lunch with two people who were professors in a Department of Environmental Studies. They described their research and the findings they presented to the government in the hopes that it would enact stricter standards to preserve the environment. Then they told me that they were surprised when their children came home from school and asked if they could start recycling things. The parents had never thought of their personal consumption patterns as contributing to environmental distress, and when they did, they began recycling immediately.

To cultivate pure activities, we imagine ourselves acting as Chenrezig acts, benefiting people in the same way that Chenrezig does. The meditation of sending out light to purify sentient beings and to give them the things they need is practicing pure activities. Here we rehearse Chenrezig's activities in our meditation. Of course, the purpose is actually to do those activities when we become capable of doing so, and visualizing doing them prepares us for this by making us familiar with an enlightened motivation and skillful means. For example, if we imagine being Chenrezig giving food to hungry sentient beings, when we next meet a street person, it will be easy to respectfully offer them some food. When we think of ourselves as Chenrezig, we'll be mindful when we do activities at our job that benefit others and we'll want to do volunteer work in our spare time.

Having pure enjoyments means we relate to the things we use in a healthy way. Instead of craving what we don't have and clinging to what we do have, we relate to objects in a balanced, respectful way. After this, it is easier to imagine that the things we contact in daily life generate bliss in us, not attachment.

In the sadhana, having pure enjoyments is exemplified by making offerings to ourselves as the deity. First we purify the offerings by dissolving the ordinary ones on the altar into emptiness. We then think that our wisdom realizing emptiness manifests as the various offering objects. For example, in the Nyung Nä sadhana, from eight BHRUM syllables appear eight huge jeweled vessels. Inside each of these an OM melts into light from which arise the eight offerings. Later in the sadhana, we offer these eight to the front generation and to ourselves as Chenrezig, each time imagining the recipient experiences great bliss that intensifies the realization of emptiness.

This is a special tantric method that enables us to use objects of enjoyment without attachment by transforming both ourselves and the objects we use. A broom becomes a beautiful object made out of light that is blissful to touch. As Chenrezig, we use it to sweep away the defilements of ourselves and others. The telephone is made from jewels and its ring is the sound of OM MANI PADME HUM. Your inbox is stacked full with sheets of mantra that you enjoy reading. When you write out a check to pay your credit card bill, think you're making offerings to the Buddha.

In this way, we view the things we encounter in daily life as enjoyments in the pure land and offer them to those around us, whom we see as Chenrezig. When using them ourselves, we offer them to ourselves as Chenrezig. When we lie down in bed, it's not "*My* comfortable bed with this cozy quilt." Rather, by touching the bed and quilt, we experience bliss free from attachment. This bliss prompts us to consider that these enjoyments are empty of inherent existence. In this way, we enjoy them without attachment. We may also pray, "May all sentient beings be able to sleep in a safe and comfortable place and awake with bodhicitta."

In this way, we transform everything we use during the day: Taking a shower is bathing in blissful nectar. Passing the ketchup becomes giving sentient beings everything they need. Eating becomes an offering to Chenrezig.

Transforming everything we use into an object in the pure land counteracts the complaining mind. During a retreat I did a few years ago, the cook served rice six times a week. I can't digest rice very well but I would think, "Never mind, so many sentient beings worked hard to make this food. I see it as blissful wisdom nectar." Then, I would eat a little and make offerings to the birds with the leftovers. I got to know the birds, which coincidentally were the same color as the deity I was meditating on. I saw the birds as the deity and imagined these deities flying in from everywhere, landing on the railing of my porch. I put out the rice transformed into blissful wisdom nectar and then made offerings to them. That helped me to transform the complaining mind that said, "Oh no, not rice again!"

Another name for Vajrayana is the Mantra Vehicle. "Mantra" means "protect the mind." Meditating on the four purities protects our mind from the 84,000 afflictions and from ordinary appearance and ordinary grasping. This is a profound and creative method to use in daily life to protect the mind from ignorance, attachment, and hostility.

In the Sutrayana approach, we meditate on an object's impermanence to lessen attachment to it or we think of its ugliness. For example, if we're attached to food, we imagine what it looks like after we've chewed it or when it's covered in mold. Because it no longer seems so desirable, our attachment to it decreases.

In the Mantra Vehicle, we make the object more beautiful, but not in a samsaric way. Instead, we dissolve it into emptiness and our blissful wisdom realizing emptiness appears in a purified form of the object. We then use enjoyments that are in the nature of blissful wisdom. In this way, using things is transformed from service to the ego into Dharma practice. We contemplate feeling blissful and generate wisdom understanding the emptiness of ourselves, the object, and the action. This method of meditation subdues attachment, hostility, and ignorance.

Sutra methods, such as those found in Lamrim and thought training, function in a slightly different way to counteract disturbing attitudes and negative emotions. For example, in sutra, meditation on patience is used to counteract anger. But in tantra, the person or situation is transformed into the deity in a pure land. We think of the irritating person who is pointing out our faults or rejecting us as Chenrezig. Then, just as we wouldn't get angry at Chenrezig, we don't waste our energy getting angry at this person either.

This does not mean, however, that we think, "This person is Chenrezig, so whatever he says must be true and whatever he does must be beneficial." Rather, we think, "He is Chenrezig, so even though he's showing this behavior, it's not real. There's not a truly existent him rejecting a truly existent me. There's no real, solid conflict. This is just an appearance. There is no inherently existent horrible person who doesn't understand me."

In general, if somebody we don't like points out our faults, our temper flares up. But if His Holiness the Dalai Lama were to say the exact same thing to us, we probably wouldn't get mad. We'd probably say, "Wow! He's right. I do have this fault," or "I did promise to do something, and then I let the person down." If His Holiness told us our faults, we wouldn't get angry. We would check our behavior and ask, "Well, did I do that?" In addition, we might even feel good because His Holiness paid attention to us and cared enough to show us how we could improve.

If we visualize the person we're in conflict with as Chenrezig, it's easier to listen to what she says. It's as if His Holiness or Chenrezig were speaking to us. Being mindful in this way helps us realize that the other person is not an inherently existent jerk. By thinking of him as empty and imagining him as Chenrezig, we're able to look at him with totally different eyes, which, in turn, transforms our experience of the situation. Imagine Chenrezig looking at you and saying, "You didn't complete this project when it was due." Instead of becoming angry, we'd be delighted to learn from this enlightened being. With delight we would examine our actions and improve them.

This is an excellent method that invites us to reflect on emptiness, to transform situations, and to open our mind and see the variety of emotional responses we could have. We don't have to respond with an automatic, predictable emotion, reacting to similar situations in the same habitual way.

The people that we tend to have conflict with or aversion for, as well as the people we're attached to, all become Chenrezig. We know Chenrezig cares for us. We know Chenrezig loves us, so we don't feel insecure and needy around him. We want to have a loving, healthy, spacious relationship with Chenrezig. Seeing the other person as Chenrezig prompts us to create a different kind of relationship with him, one imbued with care and respect.

Yet another technique to work with attachment and hostility is to imagine the person or thing we're attached to exploding into billions of atoms of Chenrezig, which absorb into us. For example, your mind is obsessing about going on vacation; you're daydreaming about it and at the same time are worried that you won't get leave from work. Visualize the vacation site—let's say a beach with attractive people, all sorts of water sports, and tables full of food. Suddenly they all dissolve into atoms of Chenrezig that absorb into you making you feel so blissful and blessed. Your mind is now content, without a trace of attachment or worry. Whether your boss gives you time off for vacation is now irrelevant, because you're totally blissful in this very moment.

II *More Meditations*

PRANAYAMA

THERE ARE TWO WAYS of cultivating the six deities. The first is by way of meditative stabilization (Skt: *dhyana*; Tib: *bsam gtan*). Here, we meditate on the six deities in sequence, gradually generating ourselves as Chenrezig. Then we remember the details of what we look like as Chenrezig: "This face is white, that one is green. This hand is holding a Dharma wheel, that hand is holding a lotus," and so on. Although we may be concentrating in the sense of not being distracted, the object we're meditating on changes—first we focus on the faces, then the implements, the garments, and so forth.

The second way of cultivating the six deities is by way of concentration (Skt: *samadhi;* Tib: *ting nge 'dzin*). Here we focus on a single object—for example, Chenrezig's body or the main face—and remain one-pointedly on that.

After meditating by way of meditative stabilization, when we meditate by way of concentration, Action Tantra's version of *pranayama* can be employed to prevent scattering and excitement and to cultivate single-pointed meditative equipoise. *Pranayama* has different meanings and entails different practices in different contexts. We have to be careful not to confuse these. Here, in Action Tantra, *prana* means "vitality" or "wind" and refers to the breath, both the air which we inhale through our nose and the winds that course through our pores and orifices. *Ayama* means "exertion," which here refers to distraction. *Ayama* can also mean "to stop the breath," because it's easier to concentrate when we hold our breath. Thus, *pranayama* is the practice of controlling the winds and distractions in order to increase our single-pointedness on the clear appearance and divine identity of the deity and thus free us from ordinary appearance and ordinary identity.

Our experience shows us that there's a relationship between the breath and the mind. When we're upset, our breathing becomes rough and our breaths short; whereas a relaxed mind is accompanied by slow, gentle breathing. When we're upset, taking a deep breath helps to calm the mind. In *pranayama* the breath is used to calm the mind and cease agitating distractions so that concentration will improve.

To control the winds and distractions, inhale through the nostrils as you normally do. At the same time gently contract the muscles surrounding your orifices. While holding the breath, think that the winds flowing through these orifices and through the pores of your body are held inside and cease moving. At this time focus on the clear appearance of yourself as Chenrezig and hold the divine identity. Because the breath, and thus the mind, are more still, it's easier to concentrate single-pointedly, without the mind wandering to other objects. When you can no longer hold your breath, gently release it. While exhaling, contemplate your Chenrezig body in general in a relaxed way. Then take another breath and hold the vitality and exertion. It's important not to strain when doing this breathing practice. In other words, don't take big, deep breaths or hold the breath until you're about ready to explode.

REPETITION IN DEPENDENCE ON THE FOUR BRANCHES

In general, until concentration on ourselves as Chenrezig becomes firm, we recite mantra to rest the mind and to develop bodhicitta through doing the various visualizations explained before. When our concentration is firm, we go on to a subtler type of mantra recitation called "mantra repetition in dependence on the four branches."

The four branches are the front deity, self-deity, mind, and sound.

The first two have been explained above. "Mind" refers to our wisdom realizing emptiness appearing in the form of a moon disk at the heart of the deity. "Sound" means the form of the mantra letters standing near the edge of the moon in the heart of the deity. The place where the moon and letters appear is in the deity in front and in oneself as the deity. These are the four branches to be mindful of while reciting the mantra.

The first repetition in dependence on the four branches is the mantra repetition observing the form of the letters in the heart of the deity in front. Here we focus on the mantra letters on the moon disk in the front Chenrezig's heart. That is, we contemplate the deity in front (or above our head), the moon at his heart, and the mantra letters on the moon. At the same time, we recite the mantra first by whispering it and then, when our mind is calmer, we do the *pranayama* practice and recite the mantra mentally while holding the breath. When we exhale in the *pranayama* practice, we observe our own divine body without reciting mantra.

The second repetition is the mantra repetition observing the form of the letters in our own heart. Here, during inhalation, we imagine the moon and mantra letters in the front deity's heart move to our heart. While contemplating ourselves as Chenrezig with the moon and mantra letters at our heart, we recite the mantra out loud in a whisper. As our concentration gets more stable, we do *pranayama* practice and recite the mantra mentally while contemplating the moon and mantra letters. Then, during exhalation, we stop reciting the mantra and contemplate the moon and mantra letters in the front Chenrezig's heart. The moving of the moon and mantra from the front Chenrezig into us and back again isn't done with every inhalation and exhalation. Rather it moves from the front deity into us during an inhalation and moves back to the front deity during an exhalation.

The third repetition in dependence on the four branches is the mantra repetition observing the sound of letters. Here we focus mainly on the sound of the mantra as if we were listening to ourselves recite it. However, we don't lose seeing ourselves as Chenrezig. That is maintained, but the primary object we focus on is the mantra sound. Here, too, we do the visualization first while reciting the mantra in a whisper and later, when the mind is more settled, while doing *pranayama* and reciting it mentally. This third repetition is subtler than the first two, so these three must be performed in order. If we meditate well, these Action Tantra meditations are very profound and lead us to progressively clearer and more stable meditative stabilizations.

MEDITATIVE STABILIZATIONS WITHOUT REPETITION

When we have some experience and mastery of the above three meditative stabilizations with repetition, we go on to three meditative stabilizations without repetition. Although these are called "without repetition," it doesn't mean without any mantra recitation at all. Rather, we recite the mantra but listen to it as if another were reciting it or as if the sound were emerging naturally without our needing to recite it. So "without repetition" means without feeling or thinking, "I am reciting the mantra." These three meditative stabilizations emphasize the cessation of self-grasping while still maintaining the conception of a conventionally existent deity. That is, while we appear in the form of Chenrezig and conceive of ourselves to be Chenrezig on the conventional level, we don't grasp at an inherently existent Chenrezig or at an inherently existent "I" that is Chenrezig.

The first meditative stabilization without repetition is the meditative stabilization of abiding in fire. We are Chenrezig, and at our heart is a moon disk upon which is a flame. Our wisdom realizing emptiness appears in the aspect of the mantra sounds within that flame. We listen as if the mantra were being recited by someone else. Our wisdom mind appears as the mantra sounds, and our mind simultaneously listens to those sounds. We do neither the whispered nor the mental recitation—because we're listening to the mantra as not being recited by us—but we may do the *pranayama*. We listen to the mantra sounds without grasping them as inherently existent.

In the previous meditations, our wisdom realizing emptiness appeared as the letters and the mantra sound, and we listened to the mantra that we recited. There was still a sense of someone who is listening and the mantra that is listened to. But here, our own mind, in dependence upon which "I" is designated, dwells within the flame, and it itself appears as the sounds being listened to within the flame. By meditating in this way, the sense of solid, fixed subject and object begins to evaporate. Doing the *pranayama* and observing the flame create the experience of bliss and warmth, which aids concentration. Through this our mind becomes powerful and our concentration stable, although we have not yet attained actual meditative quiescence (Skt: *shamatha;* Tib: *zhi gnas).* Yogis who are skilled in this meditation are not affected by hunger or thirst, and the mantra sounds reverberate continuously and simultaneously in them.

The second meditative stabilization without repetition is the meditative stabilization of abiding in sound. It resembles the first one, only our object of meditation is more subtle. At our Chenrezig heart is a moon disk with a flame, as visualized before. Upon this moon disk stands a small Chenrezig—called a wisdom being. At the heart of this tiny Chenrezig is a moon disk upon which are a HRIH and the mantra syllables, made of brilliant radiating light. They resonate with the sound of the mantra. Focus on the sound of the mantra, not as if you were reciting it, but as if the mantra were being recited by another. In other words, the sound of the mantra is naturally and effortlessly there without you reciting it. Place your concentration on that and enjoy its bliss and the peacefulness of it. Focusing on this tiny object eliminates scattering and excitement, and focusing on the bright object in the flame eliminates laxity, all of which are obstacles to meditative quiescence.

While meditating in this way, you can also do the *pranayama,* and when exhaling, observe your own Chenrezig body, but this comparatively gross or large object is not your main object of meditation; the main object of this meditative stabilization is the sound of the mantra naturally appearing at the heart of the small Chenrezig who is at your heart. The meditation abiding in sound leads to the attainment of actual meditative quiescence, which is totally free from excitement and laxity and is endowed with physical and mental pliancy and physical and mental bliss.

This meditative stabilization is blissful, clear, nondiscursive, and conjoined with the force of realizing emptiness. Yet this is not sufficient to cut the root of cyclic existence. We must still cultivate the meditative stabilization bestowing liberation at the end of sound because that concentration takes only emptiness as its object of apprehension. Only a mind realizing emptiness directly can cut the root of cyclic existence. The repetitions in dependence on the four branches, the meditative stabilization of abiding in fire, and the meditative stabilization of abiding in sound are called "yoga with signs." That is, they still have the signs of inherent existence that accompany conventional appearance. The meditative stabilization bestowing liberation at the end of sound, the third meditative stabilization without repetition, is called "yoga without signs" because it eliminates grasping at inherent existence and any signs of the false appearance of inherently existent persons and phenomena.

Before doing the meditative stabilization bestowing liberation at the end of sound, we must gain the correct view of emptiness, the Middle Way view free from the extremes of absolutism and nihilism as taught by the Prasangika Madhyamaka School. This realization of emptiness may be a correct conceptual understanding. Saying that someone has realized the correct view does not mean they have necessarily realized emptiness directly or nonconceptually. Nor does it mean they have attained the union of meditative quiescence and special insight on emptiness. Nevertheless, the wisdom which conceptually realizes emptiness produces a powerful experience that challenges our ordinary view; it is a necessary stepping stone to higher realizations.

The four-branched repetition and the meditative stabilizations of abiding in fire and in sound are done to achieve meditative quiescence, so analytical meditation on emptiness is not done during them. Rather, the main focus is stabilizing meditation on Chenrezig's body or on the mantra sound, because analytical meditation would interfere with stable concentration at this point.

Once we have completed the meditative stabilization of abiding in sound, we have attained meditative quiescence. Then we do analytical and stabilizing meditation alternately on the object of meditation, the emptiness of inherent existence. This is done until stabilizing and analytical meditation cease to interfere with each other. At the point when analytical meditation can induce pliancy and meditative quiescence on emptiness, a practitioner realizes the union of meditative quiescence and special insight on emptiness and enters the bodhisattva path of preparation.

In the meditative stabilization bestowing liberation at the end of sound, the meditation is not just conjoined with the force of realizing emptiness, but the mind of deity yoga itself realizes emptiness. Although emptiness is the main object, ourselves as Chenrezig and the mantra sounds haven't totally disappeared. That is, the deity's body and the mantra appear to the appearance factor of that mind, but only emptiness appears to the ascertainment factor of that mind. While Chenrezig and the mantra appear to that mind, that mind ascertains only emptiness. This is the union of the two truths in tantra, for one consciousness both appears in the form of the deity and the mantra (conventional truths) and simultaneously realizes emptiness (ultimate truth).

If you would like more information on these meditations, see His Holiness the Dalai Lama's book *Deity Yoga* (Snow Lion Publications). It is an excellent and more detailed guide to the repetitions in dependence on the four branches and the meditative stabilizations without repetition. Also, I highly recommend receiving detailed instructions on these meditations from a qualified tantric master.

12 *Concluding the Sadhana and Practicing in Daily Life*

MEDITATION ON THE GRADUAL PATH TO ENLIGHTENMENT (LAMRIM)

AT THE END of the mantra recitation, do some Lamrim meditation before dedicating. Lama Yeshe recommended this because our mind is calmer and clearer after meditating on Chenrezig and reciting mantra. Even if we contemplate a Lamrim topic for only ten minutes at this point, there is the possibility of experiencing its meaning more deeply than if we meditate on it without such mental preparation and purification. When our mind is clear, we can penetrate the subject more easily.

I won't go into detail here about how to do analytical and stabilizing meditation on the topics of the gradual path to enlightenment, as this is explained in many other books. However, I would like to stress the importance of doing Lamrim meditation. Nowadays, many people may hear Lamrim teachings but neglect meditation on them in favor of tantric practices. His Holiness the Dalai Lama emphasizes the value of daily meditating on the Lamrim, saying that it will make us more compassionate and wiser. Personally speaking, tantra would make no sense to me without Lamrim. When I have a problem in my life, I turn to the gradual path and to thought training for solutions. Upon their basis, applying the antidotes described in tantra are effective. Furthermore, to me, Chenrezig is a manifestation of all the Lamrim realizations. The more we understand those topics, the more we understand Chenrezig and the closer we feel to his enlightened nature.

After meditating on Lamrim, we dissolve into emptiness once more and reappear as a simple Chenrezig with one face and two arms. It is this simple form of Chenrezig that gets up from the meditation cushion and goes about the other activities in your life. As you're working, walking, eating, talking, and so forth, hold the identity of yourself as Chenrezig. Think of the beings around you as Chenrezig and the environment as a pure land. Think that the things you use and enjoy are those in a pure land and that your activities are those of Chenrezig. In this way, the four purities will shine in your mind during the break times between meditation sessions.

Although we want to maintain this pure awareness continuously, our mind slips back into its familiar ways. For this reason, we do the same sadhana in one meditation session after another. We keep meditating on emptiness, generating ourselves as Chenrezig, purifying ourselves, and enlightening all sentient beings. We do it over and over and over again. This is the meaning of "practice." Repetition is the key to transforming our minds.

DEDICATION

To conclude the sadhana, recite the dedication verses, dedicating the positive potential from your practice with a loving, compassionate attitude toward all sentient beings. You may want to imagine the positive potential (merit) radiating out in the form of light and going to all sentient beings. Remember to contemplate emptiness and dependent arising as you dedicate. You (the one who is dedicating), the positive potential being dedicated, the enlightenment you're dedicating for, the sentient beings for whose welfare you're dedicating—all these exist in dependence upon one another. All of them are merely labeled and, therefore, are empty of existing in and of themselves, from their own side. As you say the words of the dedication prayer, think that all these words are mere labels referring to things that exist by being merely labeled by words and concepts.

Also pray, "May I never be separated from Chenrezig as my actual spiritual master. Wherever I am born, may Chenrezig manifest as a perfect Mahayana and Vajrayana guru to guide me to enlightenment. May I have interest and faith in the Dharma, and may I have a good relationship with Chenrezig as my spiritual mentor. May I receive pure teachings, understand them correctly, and practice earnestly. May I also have good relationships with my Dharma friends, so that we can help, encourage, and support each other on the path. Through this, may all my lives from now until I attain full enlightenment be beneficial for all sentient beings. May I never miss an opportunity to make my life meaningful."

BREAK TIME BETWEEN SESSIONS

Try to keep an awareness of yourself as Chenrezig throughout the day, seeing the environment as the pure land and all other beings as Chenrezig. Think that even the insects are little Chenrezigs flying around. All the things you enjoy are the enjoyments of Chenrezig, all the sounds you hear are OM MANI PADME HUM, all the thoughts you think are the manifestation of Chenrezig's wisdom. By seeing everything around you in a pure way, contact with people and things produces bliss, not attachment or anger. Try to put this practice into all aspects of your life, not just into your meditation sessions. This is the meaning of practicing mindfulness when practicing Vajrayana. Mindfulness in Vajrayana is mindfulness of pure appearance and divine identity.

Seeing everyone as Chenrezig doesn't mean that everyone appears as Chenrezig with a thousand arms to your eye consciousness. Rather, it's your mental consciousness that thinks of others as Chenrezig. If we view others as a deity, then if they do something we don't like, we won't get upset with them. We still have to deal with the situation, but we won't do it with anger because who wants to get angry at Chenrezig? Similarly, if we see a good-looking person, we won't generate lust toward him or her if we think of them as Chenrezig. Why? We'd feel kind of funny getting turned on in front of a Buddha. Similarly, thinking the environment is pure doesn't mean you can throw your garbage everywhere visualizing it as lotuses in a pure land. We still have to be environmentally responsible!

Thinking of all sounds as mantra doesn't mean when someone says, "You made a mess," that you ignore the meaning of what they said and imagine they said, "OM MANI PADME HUM" instead. Rather, think of their words as vibration and recognize that no inherently existent criticism or blame exists in mere sound. That way we avoid feeling hurt or insulted by others' comments. But we should still apologize for the inconvenience we caused and rectify it.

Viewing all our thoughts and emotions as Chenrezig's wisdom doesn't mean that we let our jealousy run wild and simply say to ourselves, "This is the wisdom realizing emptiness." It means we see that the object of our jealousy and our jealousy itself lack inherent existence. Meditating on their emptiness pacifies our mind and creates a cause for our mind to become Chenrezig's.

May we all become the Great Compassionate One and benefit all sentient beings temporally and especially by leading them to full enlightenment, the total absence of all *dukkha* and the development of all good qualities.

Glossary

Affirmative phenomenon   A phenomenon realized by a mind that does not eliminate an object of negation.

Afflictions   Attitudes and emotions such as ignorance, attachment, anger, pride, jealousy, and confusion that disturb our mental peace and propel us to act in ways harmful to others.

Altruistic intention (Bodhicitta)   The mind dedicated to attaining enlightenment in order to be able to benefit all others most effectively.

Analytical meditation (Tib: *bpyad sgom*)   A type of meditation used to discern and understand the main points of a meditation topic. This may involve thinking but eventually goes beyond conceptions.

Arhat   A person who has attained liberation and is thus free from cyclic existence.

Arya   A person who has realized emptiness directly.

Attachment   An emotion that, based on exaggerating the good qualities of a person or thing, clings to it.

Basis of designation   The collection of parts or qualities in dependence upon which an object is labeled.

Bodhicitta   *See* Altruistic intention.

Bodhisattva   A person who, when seeing any sentient being, spontaneously feels the altruistic intention.

Buddha   Any person who has purified all defilements and developed all good qualities. "The Buddha" refers to Shakyamuni Buddha, who lived 2,500 years ago in India.

Buddha-nature (Buddha-potential) The factors allowing all beings to attain full enlightenment.

Compassion The wish for all sentient beings to be free from suffering and its causes.

Cyclic existence Taking uncontrolled rebirth under the influence of afflictions and karma.

Deity (Yidam) A meditational deity, one of a number of Buddhas.

Determination to be free (Renunciation) The attitude aspiring to be free from all problems and sufferings and to attain liberation.

Dharma The realizations and cessations of suffering and its causes. In a more general sense, Dharma refers to the teachings and doctrine of the Buddha.

Dukkha Unsatisfactory conditions. *See* Suffering.

Emptiness According to the Prasangika Madhyamaka School, it is the lack of independent, or inherent, existence. This is the ultimate nature or reality of all persons and phenomena.

Enlightenment (Buddhahood) The state of a Buddha, that is, the state of having forever eliminated all disturbing attitudes, karmic imprints, and their stains from one's mindstream, and having developed one's good qualities and wisdom to their fullest extent. Buddhahood supersedes liberation.

Impute To give a label or name to an object. To give meaning to an object.

Inherent or independent existence A false and nonexistent quality that we project onto persons and phenomena; existence independent of causes and conditions, parts, or the mind labeling a phenomenon.

Karma Intentional action. Our actions leave imprints on our mindstreams that bring about our experiences.

Lamrim The gradual path to enlightenment; the series of progressive topics upon which we meditate to gain deeper understanding and experience of the Buddha's teachings.

Liberation The state of having removed all afflictions and karma causing us to take rebirth in cyclic existence.

Love The wish for all sentient beings to have happiness and its causes.

Mahayana The Buddhist tradition that asserts that all beings can attain enlightenment. It strongly emphasizes the development of compassion and the altruistic intention.

Mantra A series of syllables consecrated by a Buddha and expressing the essence of the entire path to enlightenment. Mantras can be recited during meditation to calm and purify the mind.

Meditation Habituating ourselves to positive attitudes, beneficial emotions, and accurate perspectives.

Meditative quiescence The ability to remain single-pointedly on an object of meditation with a pliant and serene mind.

Nirvana The cessation of suffering and its causes. Freedom from cyclic existence.

Nonaffirming negation A negation that eliminates its object of negation but does not imply an affirmative phenomenon.

Phenomena Existent objects. This includes both permanent and impermanent existents.

Positive potential Imprints of positive actions that will result in happiness in the future.

Pure land A place established by a Buddha or bodhisattva where all conditions are conducive for practicing the Dharma and attaining enlightenment.

Real Truly or inherently existent.

Realization A deep understanding that becomes part of us and changes our outlook on the world. When we realize love, for example, the way we feel about and relate to others changes dramatically.

Sadhana The meditation practice associated with a particular Buddha. This is often a written text that one follows, by chanting or reading, in order to meditate on that Buddha.

Sangha Any person who directly and nonconceptually realizes emptiness. In a more general sense, Sangha refers to the communities of ordained monastics. It is sometimes used to refer to Buddhists in general.

Selflessness *See* Emptiness.

Special insight (Vipashyana) A wisdom thoroughly discriminating phenomena. When conjoined with meditative quiescence, it enables one to analyze the meditation object and simultaneously remain single-pointedly on it.

Spirit An unenlightened being born in the hungry ghost or demi-god (asura) realms. Spirits may be helpful or harmful.

Stabilizing meditation A type of meditation used to develop concentration. It involves training the mind to rest single-pointedly on its object of meditation.

Suffering (Dukkha) Any dissatisfactory condition. It doesn't refer only to physical or mental pain, but includes all problematic conditions.

Sutra A teaching of the Buddha; a Buddhist scripture. Sutras are found in all Buddhist traditions.

Taking refuge Entrusting one's spiritual development to the guidance of the Three Jewels—the Buddha, Dharma, and Sangha.

Tantra A scripture describing Vajrayana practice.

Thing   An impermanent phenomenon; something that performs a function.

Three higher trainings   The practices of ethics, meditative concentration, and wisdom. Practicing these three results in liberation.

Three Jewels   The Buddha, Dharma, and Sangha.

Torma   A ritual cake made out of roasted barley flour that is offered to a meditational deity.

Vajrayana   A Mahayana Buddhist tradition popular in Tibet and Japan.

Wisdom realizing emptiness   A wisdom that correctly understands the manner in which all persons and phenomena exist, that is, the mind realizing the emptiness of inherent existence.

Additional Reading

Berzin, Alexander. *Relating to a Spiritual Teacher: Building a Healthy Relationship*. Ithaca, N.Y.: Snow Lion Publications, 2000.

Chodron, Thubten. *Buddhism for Beginners*. Ithaca, N.Y.: Snow Lion Publications, 2001.

Chodron, Thubten. *How to Free Your Mind: Tara the Liberator*. Ithaca, N.Y.: Snow Lion Publications, 2005.

Chodron, Thubten. *Open Heart, Clear Mind*. Ithaca, N.Y.: Snow Lion Publications, 1990.

Chodron, Thubten. *Taming the Mind*. Ithaca, N.Y.: Snow Lion Publications, 2004.

Chodron, Thubten. *Working with Anger*. Ithaca, N.Y.: Snow Lion Publications, 2001.

Cozort, Daniel. *Highest Yoga Tantra*. Ithaca, N.Y.: Snow Lion Publications, 2005.

Dewar, Tyler, trans. *Trainings in Compassion*. Ithaca, N.Y.: Snow Lion Publications, 2004.

Dhammananda, K. Sri. *How to Live Without Fear and Worry*. Kuala Lumpur: Buddhist Missionary Society, 1989.

Dharmarakshita. *Wheel of Sharp Weapons*. Dharamsala, India: Library of Tibetan Works and Archives, 1981.

Hanh, Thich Nhat. *Being Peace*. Berkeley: Parallax Press, 1987.

H. H. Tenzin Gyatso, the Fourteenth Dalai Lama. *The Dalai Lama at Harvard*. Ithaca, N.Y.: Snow Lion Publications, 1989.

H. H. Tenzin Gyatso, the Fourteenth Dalai Lama. *Healing Anger*. Ithaca, N.Y.: Snow Lion Publications, 1997.

H. H. Tenzin Gyatso, the Fourteenth Dalai Lama. *Kindness, Clarity, and Insight*. Ithaca, N.Y.: Snow Lion Publications, 1984.

H. H. the Dalai Lama, Tsong-ka-pa, and Jeffrey Hopkins. *Deity Yoga*. Ithaca, N.Y.: Snow Lion Publications, 1981.

H. H. the Dalai Lama, Tsong-ka-pa, and Jeffrey Hopkins. *Tantra in Tibet*. Ithaca, N.Y.: Snow Lion Publications, 1987.

Hopkins, Jeffrey. *The Tantric Distinction*. Boston: Wisdom Publications, 1992.

Jampa Tegchok, Geshe. *Transforming Adversity into Joy and Courage: An Explanation of the Thirty-seven Practices of Bodhisattvas*. Ithaca, N.Y.: Snow Lion Publications, 2005.

McDonald, Kathleen. *How to Meditate*. Boston: Wisdom Publications, 1984.

Mullin, Glenn. *Path of the Bodhisattva Warrior*. Ithaca, N.Y.: Snow Lion Publications, 1988.

Rabten, Geshe, and Geshe Ngawang Dhargyey. *Advice from a Spiritual Friend*. Boston: Wisdom Publications, 1986.

Rinchen, Geshe Sonam. *The Six Perfections*. Ithaca, N.Y.: Snow Lion Publications, 1998.

Rinchen, Geshe Sonam. *The Thirty-seven Practices of Bodhisattvas*. Ithaca, N.Y.: Snow Lion Publications, 1997.

Sopa, Geshe Lhundub. *Steps on the Path to Enlightenment*. 5 volumes. Boston: Wisdom Publications, 2004-.

Thubten Yeshe, Lama. *Becoming the Compassion Buddha: Tantric Mahamudra for Everyday Life*. Boston: Wisdom Publications, 2003.

Thubten Yeshe, Lama. *Introduction to Tantra*. Boston: Wisdom Publications, 1987.

Thubten Zopa Rinpoche, Lama. *The Door to Satisfaction*. Boston: Wisdom Publications, 1994.

Thubten Zopa Rinpoche, Lama. *Transforming Problems: Utilizing Happiness and Suffering in the Spiritual Path*. Boston: Wisdom Publications, 1987.

Thubten Zopa Rinpoche, Lama, and George Churinoff. *Nyung Nä: The Means of Achievement of the Eleven-Faced Great Compassionate One, Avalokiteshvara*. Boston: Wisdom Publications, 1995

Tsong-kha-pa. *The Great Treatise on the Stages of the Path to Enlightenment*. 3 volumes. Ithaca, N.Y.: Snow Lion Publications, 2000-2004.

Tsongkhapa, Je. *The Three Principal Aspects of the Path*. Howell, N.J.: Mahayana Sutra and Tantra Press, 1988.

Wangchen, Geshe. *Awakening the Mind of Enlightenment*. Boston: Wisdom Publications, 1988.

Yangsi Rinpoche. *Practicing the Path*. Boston: Wisdom Publications, 2003.

Also see:
www.thubtenchdron.org
www.sravastiabbey.org